EQ4
DESIGN
COOKBOOK

EQ4
DESIGN
COOKBOOK

The Electric Quilt Company
419 Gould Street, Suite 2
Bowling Green, OH 43402

EQ4 Design Cookbook

Copyright © 1991-1999 by   The Electric Quilt Company
                                  419 Gould Street, Suite 2
                                  Bowling Green, OH 43402

Windows,™ Windows 95/98, and Microsoft™ are registered trademarks of Microsoft Corporation. Many titles used by manufacturers and sellers to distinguish their products are claimed as trademarks. Where The Electric Quilt Company was aware of these trademarks, the trademark symbol was printed beside the trademarked title or product name.

CONTENTS

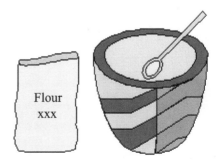

Part 1
Introduction

Part 1
Introduction

Introduction

How to Use the Cookbook

This book is not meant to be read cover to cover. Instead, it's a cookbook of step-by-step design recipes.

Maybe you won't need these recipes. Perhaps, after doing the 3 lessons in the EQ4 Getting Started book, you will "just start cooking."

But, just as you might look up a recipe for Chocolate Cake if you'd never baked from scratch, this EQ4 Design Cookbook can help you design from scratch. You'll find recipes for everything from "Making an On-Point Quilt Layout," to "Drawing an Applique Dove."

These recipes are not Lessons. Don't read them unless you want help. But if you do get stuck, find the topic in the Index, then follow the recipe directions.

Bon appetit!

About the Book Binding

Feel free to press this book open flat! And don't worry, its cloth-reinforced binding is *supposed* to be separated from the spine. It's designed to lay flat and resist cracking, no matter how flat you press it.

Part 2
Projects

Part 2
Projects

Opening an EQ3 Project

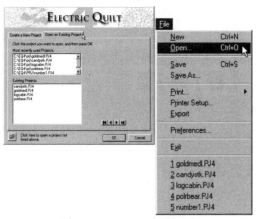

The two ways to do step 1

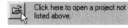

Step 2

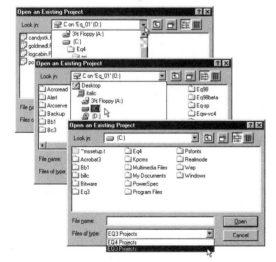

Steps 3 - 5

Opening an EQ3 Project

You can open an EQ3 (Electric Quilt version 3.0) project in EQ4. To do so, you must have the EQ3 project in your computer, or on a floppy disk.

Opening an EQ3 Project

1 Click the Open an Existing Project tab (it appears immediately when you open EQ4).
  Or
  On the FILE menu, click Open.

2 Click the folder in the bottom-left corner of the Open an Existing Project tab (marked "Click here to open a project not listed above"). This brings up a standard Windows search directory, allowing you to open a folder anywhere on your computer.

3 Click the down arrow beside the Look in box, to drop the list.

4 Scroll to find the hard drive on which EQ3 is installed (normally C:\) and click it.

5 Click the down arrow beside Files of type and choose EQ3 projects.

6 Click the project name, to select it.

7 Click the Open button.

Creating a New Project

Creating a New Project When Opening EQ4

1 Start EQ4. (Double-click EQ4's desktop icon, or open EQ4 from the Start and Programs' menus.)

2 On the EQ4 opening screen's "Create a New Project" tab, type any name you would like.

3 Click OK. The opening screen will disappear. You will be on the quilt or block worktable.

4 At this point you can work on as many different blocks or quilts as you want.

5 Click the Save in Sketchbook button for each block or quilt you want to keep. Whatever you've been working on saves to the Sketchbook.

6 Click the Save button to save your Sketchbook contents permanently.

7 In the top right corner click the "X" to close the program. You will receive a message, "Save changes to *(the name of your project)?"*

8 Click Yes. The program will close with your new project saved.

Creating a New Project When in EQ4

If you decide to create a project once you're in EQ4, whether you have another project open (go to step 1), or you're in EQ4 without working on a project (go to step 2), there's no problem.

1 If you're working in another project, click the Save in Sketchbook button.

2 Click the Create a New project button.

3 On the Create a New Project tab, type the name of a new project.

4 Click OK. The worktable will open to

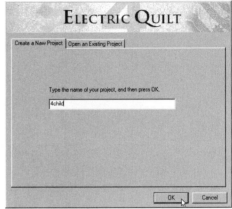

Steps 2 and 3

Step 5   *Step 6*   *Step 7*

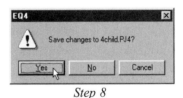

Step 8

Step 1   *Step 2*

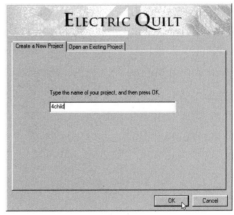

Steps 3 and 4

begin your new project. If you were working on another project and saved it in the Sketchbook you will receive a message, "Save changes to *(the name of your project)?*" Click Yes.

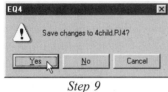

Step 6

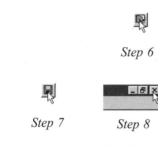

Step 7   *Step 8*

Step 9

5   At this point you can work on as many different blocks or quilts as you want.

6   Click the Save in Sketchbook button for each block or quilt you want to keep. Whatever you've been working on saves to the Sketchbook.

7   Click the Save button.

8   In the top-right corner click the "X" to close the program. You will receive a message, "Save changes to *(the name of your project)?*"

9   Click Yes. The program will close with your new project saved.

Notes & Tips ────────────

- **Whether you see the quilt or block worktable open up when you start EQ4 depends what you used the last time EQ4 was open. If this is your first time starting EQ4 the quilt worktable will appear.**

- **You must save whatever you're working on in the Sketchbook or it will not get saved in your project (even if you click on the Save button).**

- **To open one of your newly created projects see:** OPENING A PROJECT.

Creating a New Project

Opening a Project

Opening a project puts the blocks and quilts you've saved in that project back into the Sketchbook.

Opening a Project Saved in EQ4

1   Click the Open an Existing Project tab (it appears immediately when you open EQ4).

   OR

   On the FILE menu, click Open.

2   Click on the project you want to open. (Click on either the top or bottom list. The top list shows the last five projects opened. The bottom list shows all projects saved in EQ4.)

   You will see a quilt if your project contains quilts. To see all the quilts in the project, click the forward and back arrows.

3   Click OK. The Open box will close. Your project will open and appear in the Sketchbook.

Opening a Project Saved on a Floppy Disk

1   Click the folder in the bottom-left corner of the Open an Existing Project tab (marked "Click here to open a project not listed above"). This brings up a standard Windows search directory, allowing you to open a folder anywhere on your computer.

2   Insert the floppy disk containing the project into your floppy drive.

3   Click the down arrow beside the Look in box, to drop the list.

4   Scroll to find your floppy drive (A:\ or B:\) and click it.

5   Click the project name, to select it.

Note:
If you do not see a project name, the project on the floppy may be an EQ3 project.

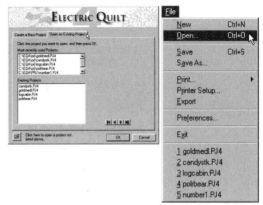

The two ways to do step 1

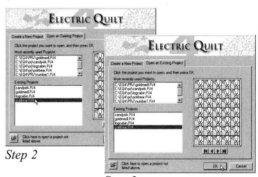

Step 2

Step 3

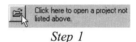

Step 1

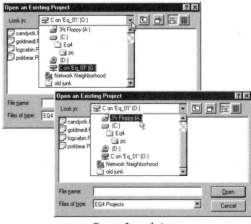

Steps 3 and 4

6 Optional: To open an EQ3 project, click the down arrow by Files of type. Click EQ3 Projects.

7 Click the Open button.

 Notes & Tips ————————————————

• **If you can't find a project, you can use the Windows Find Files or Folders feature to find it.**
1 At the Win 95/98 Start button click Start – Find – Files or Folders.
2 Type *.PJ4
3 Click Find Now.
All EQ4 projects on your computer will be listed. Find the project name you're seeking. Write down whatever is in the "In Folder" for this project. Then look for this drive and folder when you follow the directions, above, for opening your project.

Opening a Project

Opening a Project Sent by E-mail

If necessary, consult your e-mail software documentation. In order to find any project sent to you by e-mail, you will first need to know where (which hard drive and which folder) messages go when you download them into your computer. Then do the following steps.

1 Click the Open an Existing Project tab (it appears immediately when you open EQ4).

   OR

   On the FILE menu, click Open.

2 Click the folder in the bottom-left corner of the Open an Existing Project tab (marked "Click here to open a project not listed above"). This brings up a standard Windows search directory, allowing you to open a folder anywhere on your computer.

3 Click the down arrow beside the Look in box, to drop the list.

4 Scroll to find the hard drive on which your e-mail software is installed (normally C:\) and click it.

5 Scroll to find the folder for your e-mail program and click it. If your e-mail documentation tells you another folder name, find it here and open it.

6 If the e-mailed project was made in EQ3, then click the down arrow beside Files of type and choose EQ3 projects.

7 Click the project name, to select it.

8 Click the Open button.

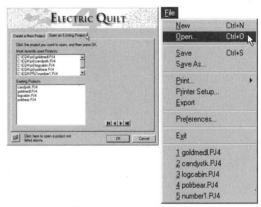

The two ways to do step 1

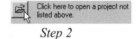

Step 2

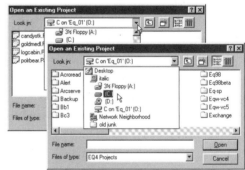

Steps 3 and 4

Saving a Project to a Disk

Step 3

Step 4

Step 7

Step 8

Once you have designs in your Sketchbook, you can save them to your computer's hard drive or to a floppy disk. Here is how to save the project to a floppy.

1   Put a formatted floppy disk into your computer's floppy drive.

2   You must have designs in your Sketchbook. If you have the Sketchbook open, click the (X) Close button to close the Sketchbook.

3   On the FILE menu, click Save As. The Save As box appears.

4   Look at the File name window. The name is highlighted (blue). If the name says Project1, it means your project (unnamed) will be named Project1 unless you rename it.

5   To rename the project, type a new name. The name Project1 will disappear as you type.

6   Click the down arrow beside the Save in window to drop the list of choices.

7   Click 3 ½ Floppy (A).

Note:
If your floppy drive has another letter name, click that letter.

8   Click the Save button. Your project will be saved on the floppy disk. (You won't see anything happen.)

Note:
To open a project from a floppy disk see:
OPENING A PROJECT.

Saving a Project

When you save a project, all quilts and blocks in your Sketchbook get saved permanently on the hard drive.

Once saved, a project can't change unless you open it again, make changes, and save again.

Saving a New Block or Quilt to an Existing Project

This section assumes that you've already opened a project, new or existing.

Step 1

1   Click the Save in Sketchbook button. You'll see the flash of a moving bar at screen bottom, indicating that the quilt or block you're working on will be saved to the Sketchbook.

Step 2

2   Click the Save button. You will not see anything happen. But your Sketchbook contents are now saved permanently.

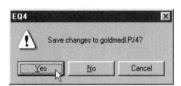

3   Repeat the above two steps as you make new designs. When you are ready to exit the program, click on the "X" in the top-right corner. You will receive a message asking, "Save changes to *(the name of your project)*?" Click Yes to save the project and close the program.

Step 3

Saving a New Block or Quilt When a Project Does Not Exist

Suppose you open the program without starting a new project, or opening an existing project. Then, later, you design something you'd like to save. Here's what to do to start a new project after you already have something in your Sketchbook.

1   Click the Save in Sketchbook button. You'll see the flash of a moving bar at screen bottom, indicating that the quilt or block you're working on will be saved to the Sketchbook.

Step 1

2   Click the Save button. The Save As pop-up

Step 2

Saving a Project

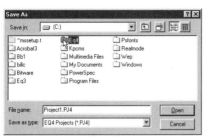

Step 3

Step 4

Step 5

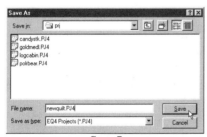

Step 7

menu will appear. Since you don't have an open project, you will need to direct and name a new project.

3 You will see your hard drive (most likely "C") in the Save As dialog box with program folders underneath. Locate and double-click the EQ4 folder. Now EQ4 will be in the Save As dialog box.

4 Double-click the PRJ folder. This puts it into the Save in box.

5 Look at the Filename box. If a project name appears there, you need to erase it and type a new name. To do so, either highlight the name (click, hold and drag your cursor across the name) and type a new project name, or click to place your cursor behind the name, backspace to erase it, and type your new name.

6 Click Save. Your blocks and quilts are now saved in a project.

7 At this point, since you have a project open, if you make new designs that you want to save to the project you simply click Save in Sketchbook, and then the Save button.

 Notes & Tips

- **To open your project again see:** OPENING A PROJECT.
- **You must save whatever you're working on in the Sketchbook or it will not get saved in your project (even if you click the Save button).**
- **If you forget to rename your project the program will save it as Project1.PJ4. You can rename the project. See:** RENAMING A PROJECT.
- **You can add a new folder within the Project folder by clicking on the "Create a New Folder" icon. This is helpful when sorting many projects.**

Saving a Project

15

Renaming a Project

It is very simple to rename a project, whether you forgot to originally name it, or you want to change the existing name.

1 You must be at EQ4's opening screen with two tabs. If you start EQ4 it will be the first screen that appears. (If you are already in the program, click the Open a project button.)

2 Click the Open an Existing Project tab.

3 Click the folder icon in the bottom-left corner. You will be in the Open an Existing Project pop-up menu with the Prj folder in the Look in box.

4 Underneath the Look in box are projects saved in the Prj folder. Click the name of the project you want to change. (The name will then appear highlighted or darker.)

5 Click the project name again. The name, still highlighted will now have a box surrounding it.

6 Begin typing a new project name. The previous name will disappear as you type.

7 Be sure to type ".PJ4" after the new name so your project will appear in the projects folder.

8 Click Open to open your project, or Cancel to go back to EQ4's opening screen.

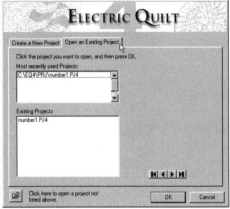

Step 2

Step 3

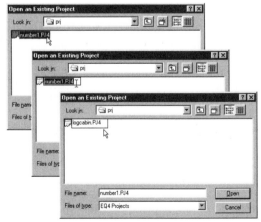

Steps 4, 5 and 6

 Notes & Tips

- **If you do not see your project listed in the Open an Existing Project pop-up menu under the Look in box, see:** OPENING A PROJECT **(to locate your project).**
- **If you click Cancel after renaming the project, you will not see the change until the next time you open the project.**

Deleting a Project

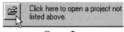

Step 2

Step 3

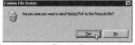

Step 5

Step 6

1   Click on the Open a project button.   The EQ4 Project pop-up menu will appear with the Open an Existing Project tab on top.

2   Click on the open folder icon (that reads, "Click here to open a project not listed above.") at the bottom left corner. The Windows project pop-up menu will appear with EQ4 projects listed under the prj folder.

3   Click on the project name you want to delete so it is highlighted (darker).

4   Press the DELETE key. A Confirm File Delete pop-up menu will appear making sure you want to send the project to the recycling bin.

5   Click the Yes button if you want to delete the project. (Click No if you don't want to delete the project.) The project name will disappear from the Windows project pop-up menu.

6   Click on Cancel. You will return to EQ4's project pop-up menu where your deleted project name will still appear. However, the project name will be gone the next time you open this menu. (If you try to open the project you will receive a message that it cannot be found.)

7   Click on Cancel. You will return to your quilt or block worktable.

💡 **Notes & Tips** ──────────────

• **Make sure you want to delete an entire project instead of an individual block or quilt. To delete a separate quilt, block, or fabric see:** DELETING QUILTS, BLOCKS, OR FABRICS.

Deleting a Project

17

Part 3
Quilts

Part 3
Quilts

Making a Quilt Layout

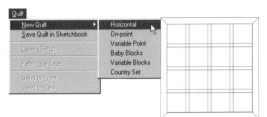

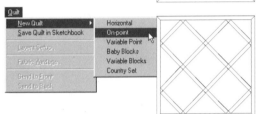

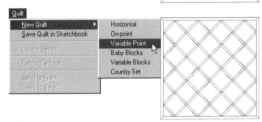

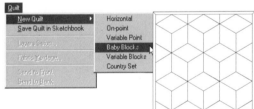

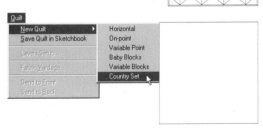

1 On the WORKTABLE menu, click Work on Quilt.

2 On the QUILT menu, point to New Quilt, click the layout style you prefer.

Horizontal - Horizontal layouts arrange blocks in horizontal and vertical rows. Blocks can be rectangular or square. The layout can include optional sashing, corner blocks and a sash border.

On-Point - On-point layouts contain square blocks tipped 45 degrees so they appear as diamonds.

Variable Point - Variable-point layouts are identical to on-point, except blocks can have a different width and height.

Baby Blocks - Baby Blocks layouts are overall grids of 3-D cubes made with diamonds with equal sides.

Variable Blocks - Variable Blocks layouts are like baby blocks, but with blocks that can have unequal sides and angles.

Country Set - Country Set layouts provide a large central area for placing blocks of different sizes. You can vary the height and width of this central area. Blocks can be placed anywhere inside of the center. Alignment of blocks is up to you. Blocks can be any size and can overlap each other.

3 Click the Layout tab. Adjust the layout to choose number and size of blocks and other options. For more information see:

MAKING A HORIZONTAL QUILT LAYOUT

MAKING AN ON-POINT QUILT LAYOUT

MAKING A VARIABLE POINT QUILT LAYOUT

MAKING A BABY BLOCKS QUILT LAYOUT

MAKING A VARIABLE BLOCKS QUILT LAYOUT

MAKING A COUNTRY SET QUILT LAYOUT

Making a Horizontal Quilt Layout

1 On the WORKTABLE menu, click Work on Quilt.

2 On the QUILT menu, point to New Quilt, click Horizontal.

3 Click the Layout tab.

4 In Number of Blocks, click the up and down arrows beside Horizontal and Vertical to make the number of blocks you want, from 1 x 1 to 48 x 48.

5 In Size of blocks, click, hold, and drag the Width and Height slider bars to make the block size you want, from 1.00" to 48.00".

Note:
> Slider bar shortcuts – click right on the bar (not the slider rectangle). This "jumps" the slider bar ¼" with each click.
>
> **OR**
>
> Click, hold, and drag your cursor across the size number, to highlight it, then type the size you want.

6 In Sashing, click, hold, and drag the slider bar to make the sash size you want, from .25" to 10.00". For no sash, make the sash size 0.00".

7 Click the Borders tab.

If you do *not* want a border, make all read 0.00.

If you *do* want one or more borders, see:
MAKING QUILT BORDERS.

💡 **Notes & Tips** _____

• You can easily move the slider bars in 1/4 inch increments by clicking on the slider bar, then using your keyboard right or left arrow keys.

Step 1

Step 2

Step 3

Steps 4–6

Step 7

Every time you click on a bar, you gain ¼".

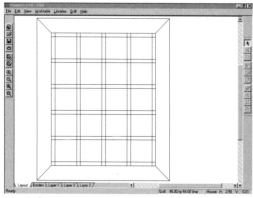

A finished quilt layout - yours may look different, depending on your choices.

Making an On-Point Quilt Layout

Step 1

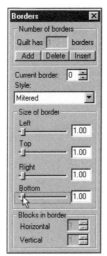

Step 2

Steps 4–6

Step 7

1 On the WORKTABLE menu, click Work on Quilt.

2 On the QUILT menu, point to New Quilt, click On-Point. An on-point layout style appears.

3 Click the Layout tab.

4 In Number of Blocks, click the up and down arrows beside Horizontal and Vertical to make the number of blocks you want, from 1 x 1 to 48 x 48.

5 In Size of Blocks, click, hold, and drag the slider bar to make the block size you want, from 1.00" to 48.00".

Note:
Slider bar shortcuts – click right on the bar (not the slider rectangle). This "jumps" the slider bar ¼" with each click.

OR

Click, hold, and drag your cursor across the size number, to highlight it, then type the size you want.

6 In Sashing, click, hold, and drag the slider bar to make the sash size you want, from .25" to 10.00". For no sash, make the sash size 0.00".

7 Click the Borders tab.

If you do *not* want a border, then, make all read 0.00.

If you *do* want one or more borders, see:
MAKING QUILT BORDERS.

Now you may want to see:
SETTING BLOCKS INTO A QUILT LAYOUT
SETTING PLAIN BLOCKS INTO A QUILT LAYOUT

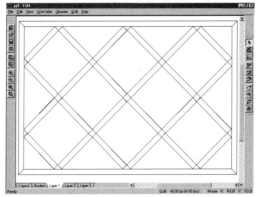

The finished quilt layout

Making a Variable Point Quilt Layout

1   On the WORKTABLE menu, click Work on Quilt.

2   On the QUILT menu, point to New Quilt, click Variable Point. A variable point layout style appears.

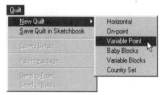

Step 1

Step 2

3   Click on the Layout tab.

4   In Number of Blocks, click on the up and down arrows to make the number of blocks you want, from 1 x 1 to 48 x 48.

Note:
Variable point layouts are identical to on-point layouts except that blocks can have different width and height.

5   In Size of Blocks, click, hold, and drag the Width and Height slider bars to make the block size you want, from 1.00" to 48.00".

Note:
The width and height measurements in this layout style refer to the horizontal and vertical dimensions of the block (so measure diagonally across the diamond).

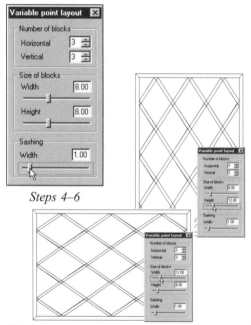

Steps 4–6

6   In Sashing, click, hold, and drag the slider bar to make the sash size you want, from .25" to 10.00". For no sash, make the sash size 0.00" (0.00cm).

7   Click on the Borders tab.

If you do *not* want a border, then, in Size of border, click, hold, and drag the Left, Top, Right and Bottom slider bars until they all read 0.00.

If you *do* want one or more borders, see:
MAKING QUILT BORDERS.

Now you may want to see:
SETTING BLOCKS INTO A QUILT LAYOUT
SETTING PLAIN BLOCKS INTO A QUILT LAYOUT

Changing the width and/or height settings will change the appearance greatly.

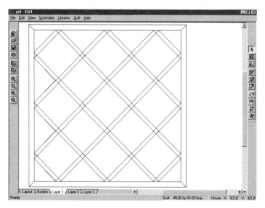

The finished quilt layout

Making a Variable Blocks Quilt Layout

Step 1

Step 2

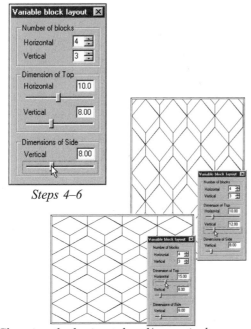

Steps 4–6

Changing the horizontal and/or vertical settings will change the appearance greatly.

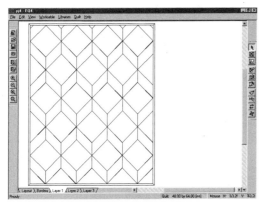

The finished quilt layout

1 On the WORKTABLE menu, click Work on Quilt.

2 On the QUILT menu, point to New Quilt, click Variable Blocks. A variable blocks layout style appears.

3 Click the Layout tab.

4 In Number of Blocks, click on the up and down arrows to make the number of blocks you want, from 1 x 1 to 48 x 48.

Note: Variable blocks layouts are like baby blocks layouts. The difference is that variable blocks layouts can have unequal sides and angles. Experiment by sliding the slider bars that control block dimensions and you'll see what great variety this layout style provides.

5 In Dimension of Top, click, hold, and drag both the Horizontal and Vertical slider bars from 1.00" to 48.00" to make the block top the size you want.

6 In Dimension of side, click, hold, and drag the slider bar to make the block side the size you want, from 1.00" to 48.00".

Note:
Slider bar shortcuts – click right on the bar (not the slider rectangle). This "jumps" the slider bar ¼" with each click.

OR

Click, hold, and drag your cursor across the size number, to highlight it, then type the size you want.

7 Click the Borders tab.

If you do *not* want a border, make all read 0.00.

If you *do* want one or more borders, see:
MAKING QUILT BORDERS.

Now you may want to see:
SETTING BLOCKS INTO A QUILT LAYOUT
SETTING PLAIN BLOCKS INTO A QUILT LAYOUT

Making a Variable Blocks Quilt Layout

Making a Baby Blocks Quilt Layout

1 On the WORKTABLE menu, click Work on Quilt.

Step 1

2 On the QUILT menu, point to New Quilt, click Baby Blocks. A baby blocks layout style appears.

3 Click the Layout tab.

Step 2

4 In Number of Blocks, click the up and down arrows to make the number of blocks you want, from 1 x 1 to 48 x 48.

5 In Size of Blocks, click, hold, and drag the Horizontal and Vertical slider bars to make the block size you want, from 1.00" to 48.00".

Note:
Slider bar shortcuts – click right on the bar (not the slider rectangle). This "jumps" the slider bar ¼" with each click.

OR

Click, hold, and drag your cursor across the size number, to highlight it, then type the size you want.

Steps 4–5

6 Click the Borders tab.

If you do *not* want a border, then, in Size of border make all read 0.00.

Step 6

If you *do* want one or more borders, see:
MAKING QUILT BORDERS.

Now you may want to see:
SETTING BLOCKS INTO A QUILT LAYOUT
SETTING PLAIN BLOCKS INTO A QUILT LAYOUT

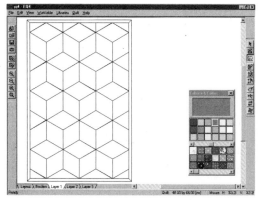

The finished quilt layout

Making a Country Set Quilt Layout

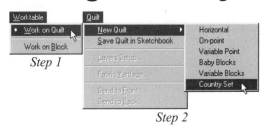

Step 1

Step 2

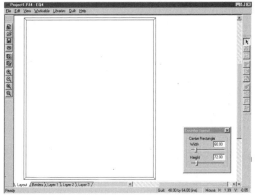

Step 3

Unlike the other quilt layouts, there are very few options for the country set quilt.

Country Set layouts can be filled with large and small blocks together in one quilt. "Country Set" is simply our name for this layout style that starts out as a large blank space. You can fill this space with any blocks, any size, anywhere on your quilt.

All other layout styles have shortcuts letting you fill the layout quickly. No shortcuts are possible with Country Set, because anything goes! You create a custom layout by setting each block exactly as you want it.

1   On the WORKTABLE menu, click Work on Quilt.

2   On the QUILT menu, point to New Quilt, click Country Set.

3   Click the Layout tab. A large open layout appears. There are no block spaces marked, because you can set blocks anywhere, and in any size, on this layout.

Important:
   You must decide on the overall size of your quilt, borders included, *before* you begin setting blocks into a Country Set layout. You will mess up your quilt design if you change the size of the quilt (by adding a border, for example) after blocks are set.

See: SETTING BLOCKS INTO A COUNTRY SET QUILT

Making a Country Set Quilt Layout

Making Quilt Borders

To work on borders, you must first have a quilt layout. If you do not have a layout showing on the worktable, start at step 1 below. If you do have a layout, start at step 3.

Step 1

Step 2
For our example, we'll be using a Horizontal layout.

1 On the WORKTABLE menu, click Work on Quilt.

2 On the QUILT menu, point to New Quilt, click any layout style. Then to make a quilt border, follow the steps below.

Step 1

3 Click the Borders tab. The Borders box will appear.

4 In Number of Borders, click the Add button to add a border. You can add up to 48 borders. The added border will be mitered, but you can change the style.

To change a border style

5 Click the quilt border you want to change. The border turns gray, showing it is selected.

6 Click the down arrow on the Style box. A list of border style choices drops down.

7 Click your style choice.

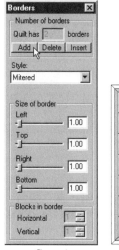

Note:
If you choose a style that can have blocks in it, then the Blocks in border number boxes will light up, below. Click the Horizontal and Vertical arrows to select the block number you want. Border blocks must fit in the border style and size you have selected.

Step 4   *Step 5*

Border Size

8 To change a border size, under Size of Border, click, hold, and drag the Left, Top, Right, Bottom slider bars. Each border side can have a different width.

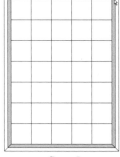
Step 6

💡 **Notes & Tips** ─────────────

• There are eleven border styles. Each border

Making Quilt Borders

can be a different style, but all four sides of a border must be the same style. See: QUILT BORDER EXAMPLES.

- To delete a border, click the quilt border you want to delete. The border turns gray, showing it is selected. Press your keyboard DELETE key.

- To insert a border between another, click the quilt border you want to insert a border in front of. The border turns gray, showing it is selected. Click the Insert button. A mitered border will be inserted. To change the border style, do steps 6 & 7 above.

- You can place, rotate and flip blocks in a border just as in a quilt.

Making Quilt Borders

Quilt Border Examples

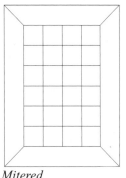 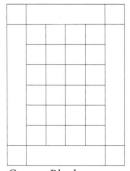 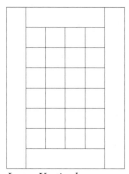 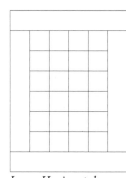

Mitered　　*Corner Blocks*　　*Long Vertical*　　*Long Horizontal*

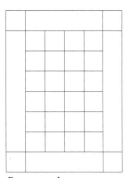 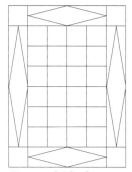 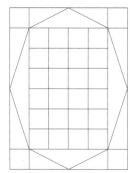 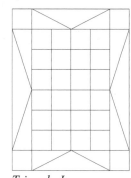

*Rectangular
Blocks*　　*Diamond Blocks*　　*Triangle Out*　　*Triangle In*

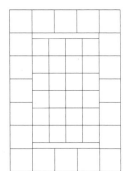 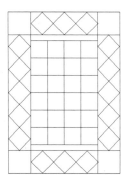 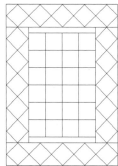

Tile Squares　　*Tile On Point*　　*Tile On Point
Corners*

30

Saving Blocks/Quilts in the Sketchbook

Step 1

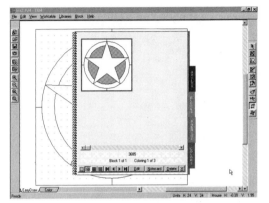

After pressing the Save in Sketchbook button, you can see your block (or quilt) in the Sketchbook.

Saving blocks or quilts in the Sketchbook saves them temporarily.

Once something is in your Sketchbook you can then save it permanently by saving your project on the hard drive.

If you get a block from the Block Library, the block automatically goes into your Sketchbook. But if you draw your own block, or make a quilt, you must save it in the Sketchbook yourself.

1 Once your block or quilt is on the screen, click the Save in Sketchbook button. A progress bar will appear along the screen bottom, indicating saving in the Sketchbook.

 Notes & Tips

- To see the Sketchbook, click the View Sketchbook button 🖻 (or press the F8 key).
- You can save as many items as you want in the Sketchbook. You can save notes about quilts or blocks. (See: KEEPING DESIGN NOTES.)
- To retrieve a block from the Sketchbook, so you can work on it again, click the block in the Sketchbook, then click the Edit button.
- To retrieve a quilt from the Sketchbook, click the forward or back arrows until you see the quilt you want, then click the Edit button.
- To delete a block or quilt from the Sketchbook, click the block (or have the quilt showing) in the Sketchbook, then click the Delete button.
- To close the Sketchbook, click the (X) Close button (or press the ESC key).

Getting Blocks/Quilts from the Sketchbook

If you want to get a block or quilt out of the Sketchbook and back down to the worktable (perhaps to print it, or to redesign it), here's how. These steps assume you have a block or quilt already in the Sketchbook.

1   Click the View Sketchbook button. The Sketchbook opens.

2   Click the Blocks tab to view the blocks; click the Quilts tab to view the quilts.

3   Click right on the block you want; if you have more than one quilt, click the forward arrow to page through the quilts until you see the one you want.

4   Click the Edit button. The quilt or block you selected will be back down on the worktable with the proper tools.

Step 1

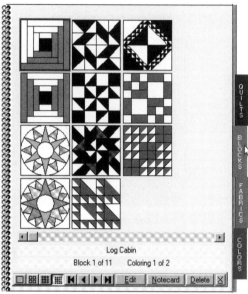

Step 2

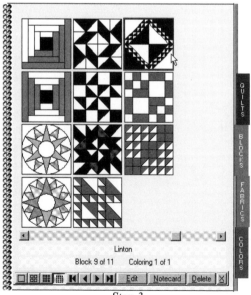

Step 3

Step 4

Coloring Blocks in a Quilt

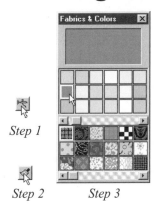

Step 1

Step 2   *Step 3*   *Step 4*

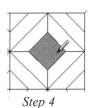

You can color blocks right on the quilt. (This works whether your blocks are line drawings, or blocks from the Block Library.)

1 To color on a quilt you must first have a quilt set with blocks.

See: MAKING A QUILT LAYOUT; SETTING BLOCKS INTO A QUILT LAYOUT.

Coloring a quilt one patch at a time

2 Click the Paintbrush tool. The Fabrics & Colors palette will appear.

3 Click on a fabric (patterned) or a color (solid) swatch.

4 Click on a patch in any block. It will change to your selected color.

Note:
For a detailed description of using the Paintbrush tool, see: COLORING A BLOCK.

Coloring multiple patches

1 Click the Spraycan tool. The Fabrics & Colors palette will appear.

2 Click on any patch in any colored block.

3 Click any color or fabric swatch in the palette. This "spray" paints the selected patches in any one block instantly.

Step 2

Tip:
CTRL + click = Holding down the CTRL key and clicking on any patch will color all identical, similarly colored patches in the quilt.

ALT + click = Holding down the ALT key and clicking on any patch will color all identical, similarly colored patches in alternate blocks in the quilt.

Notes & Tips ─────────

• You can also use the Swap tool to change color over the whole quilt.

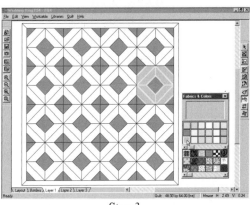

Step 3

Setting Plain Blocks into a Quilt Layout

To set plain blocks of color or fabric into your layout (rather than pieced or appliqued blocks), use the Plain Block tool. Have a quilt layout on the screen and begin at step 6. (Or, to make a quilt layout, follow steps 1-5 below.)

Step 1

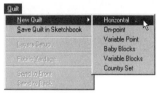

Step 2

1   On the WORKTABLE menu, click Work on Quilt.

2   On the QUILT menu, point to New Quilt, click the layout style you prefer. See: MAKING A QUILT LAYOUT.

3   Click the LAYOUT tab. Adjust the layout to choose number and size of blocks and other options. See: MAKING A HORIZONTAL QUILT LAYOUT; MAKING AN ON-POINT QUILT LAYOUT; MAKING A VARIABLE-POINT QUILT LAYOUT; MAKING A BABY BLOCKS QUILT LAYOUT; or, MAKING A VARIABLE BLOCKS QUILT LAYOUT.

4   Click the Borders tab. Adjust the border, choosing the number, style, and size of borders. See: MAKING QUILT BORDERS.

5   Click Layer 1. You will see your quilt layout.

6   Click the Plain Block tool.

   The Fabrics & Colors palette will appear. Your cursor will look like a box with a downward arrow coming out of the left side.

7   Click on a color or fabric swatch from the palette. (Click, hold, and drag on the slider bar to see all swatches.)

8   Point the arrow tip of the cursor to the part of the quilt you want to color and click. Your block will fill with a plain block of color or fabric.

9   Continue clicking on swatches, and then your quilt, until you're done coloring.

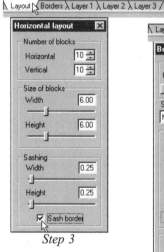

Step 3

Step 4

Step 5

Step 7

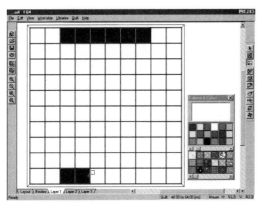

Using the Plain Block tool, we've painted a
few Plain Blocks.

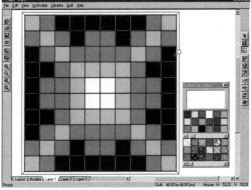

A finished quilt

 Notes & Tips

- You can use the Paintbrush tool to color.
- You can color using other fabrics or colors.

See:

CREATING NEW COLORS

GETTING FABRICS FROM THE LIBRARY

MAKING PRINT FABRICS IN NEW COLORWAYS

COLORING BLOCKS IN A QUILT

Setting Blocks into a Quilt Layout

Once you have blocks in your Sketchbook, and a quilt layout showing, you can design a quilt by setting blocks into the layout. If you already have a layout and blocks, start below at step 7. If you don't have a layout or blocks, start at step 1.

Step 1

Step 2

1   On the WORKTABLE menu, click Work on Quilt.

2   On the QUILT menu, point to New Quilt, click the layout style you prefer. (See: MAKING A QUILT LAYOUT)

3   Click the Layout tab. Adjust the layout to choose number and size of blocks and other options. See: MAKING A HORIZONTAL QUILT LAYOUT; MAKING AN ON-POINT QUILT LAYOUT; MAKING A VARIABLE-POINT QUILT LAYOUT; MAKING A BABY BLOCKS QUILT LAYOUT; or, MAKING A VARIABLE BLOCKS QUILT LAYOUT.

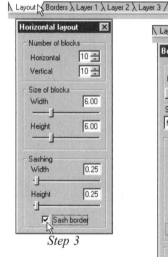

Step 3

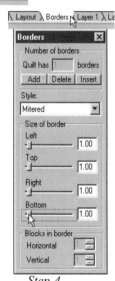

Step 4

4   Click the Borders tab. Adjust the border, choosing the number, style, and size of borders. See: MAKING QUILT BORDERS.

5   Click Layer 1. You will see your quilt layout.

6   Get quilt blocks from the Block Library. See: GETTING BLOCKS FROM THE LIBRARY OR Draw quilt blocks and save them in the Sketchbook.

Step 5

7   Click on the Set tool. ⊞ This will open the Sketchbook Blocks pop-up menu and show you the blocks you have copied.

8   Click on any block in your Sketchbook to select it.

Tip:
Whether you copied the block when it was a line drawing, in grayscale, or color from the library, you can view all of those variations from the sketchbook. Click on the color arrows and you will see all 3 "colorways." You can recolor any block whether you set it in a quilt as a line drawing or as a colored block.

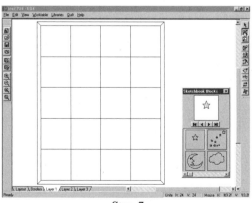

Step 7

Setting Blocks into a Quilt Layout

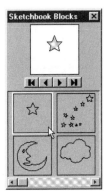

Step 8

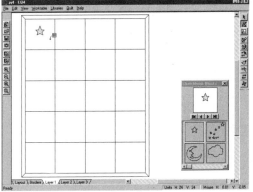

Step 9

9 Point your mouse cursor to a block space in the layout and click. The selected block will pop into the quilt. (You can also set blocks into sashes, sash corners and border block spaces by clicking.)

💡 **Notes & Tips** ────────────

- **To set the same block into all quilt spaces at once – use** CTRL **+ click. (Hold down the** CTRL **key and click on the quilt.)**
- **To set the same block into every other space – use** ALT **+ click.**
- **To rotate or flip blocks see:** ROTATING OR FLIPPING BLOCKS
- **To color blocks see:** COLORING BLOCKS IN A QUILT
- **To set plain squares of color see:** SETTING PLAIN BLOCKS INTO A QUILT LAYOUT
- **To remove a block from the layout, immediately after you've set it, choose Undo from the Edit menu.**
- **To replace one block with another, just set one block on top of the other.**

Setting Blocks into a Quilt Layout

Setting Blocks into a Country Set Quilt

Country Set layouts let you combine large and small blocks, square, rectangular or on-point, together in one quilt. You start out with a large blank space. You fill this space, setting each block exactly as you want it, until the space is filled to create your quilt. Have a Country Set layout on your worktable and start at step 3. Or, if you do not have a layout, start at step 1.

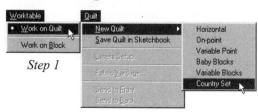

Step 1

Step 2

1   On the WORKTABLE menu, click Work on Quilt.

2   On the QUILT menu, point to New Quilt, click Country Set.

3   Click the Layout tab. A large open layout appears. There are no block spaces marked, because you can set blocks anywhere, and in any size, on this layout. Choose the Width and Height you want for the main body of your quilt.

Step 3

4   Click the Borders tab. Choose the border number, size and styles you want to set up your overall layout size and style.

Step 4

Note:

> Important — You must decide on the overall size of your quilt, borders included, *before* setting blocks into a Country Set layout. Changes to layout or border size after blocks are set will make all blocks shift on the quilt. Therefore always finalize overall quilt layout, including borders, before setting blocks into a Country Set quilt. No other quilt layout styles require this.

5   Click the Layer 1 tab. You will see your quilt layout.

Step 5

6   Get blocks from the Block Library. See: GETTING BLOCKS FROM THE LIBRARY. OR Draw quilt blocks and save them in the Sketchbook.

Setting a Block

7   Click the Set tool. This will open the Sketchbook Blocks pop-up menu and show you the blocks you have copied.

Step 7

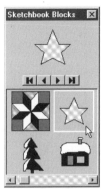

Step 8

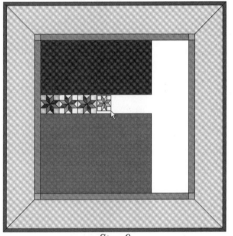

Step 9

A finished Country Set quilt

8 Click any block in your Sketchbook to select it.

9 Pointing to your quilt, drag the mouse to form a box. The selected block will pop into the box when you release the mouse.

Note:

To replace one block for another in the quilt, click the MIDDLE of the existing block (on the quilt).

To set a block of a certain size, shape or rotation, choose Layers Options on the QUILT menu, make selections on the Layer 1 tab, click OK, then hold down your keyboard SHIFT key as you drag a block from the Sketchbook Blocks pop-up to the quilt. A select box forms as you drag. The block pops into the quilt when you release the mouse button. The block shape, size and orientation are set by your selections in the Layers 1 box.

"Square" blocks remain square even when resized.

"Rectangle" blocks can be resized as any rectangle.

"Diamond" blocks will automatically set on point.

"O" orientation means the block will be set normally, without extra rotation. Rotation angle is measured in degrees, increasing clockwise. Minimum value -90; maximum value +90. For more information on "Snap" and "Snap spacing" see the on screen Help files in EQ4.

Moving and Resizing a Block

10 Click the Adjust tool.

11 Click the block on your quilt. A resize box, with corner nodes, forms around the block.

12 To move the block, point at the block's center, then drag the mouse. To resize the block, point at a corner node and drag.

Notes & Tips

• To delete a block, click the Adjust tool, click on the block, press the DELETE key.

• All quilt tools work on Country Set, so you can rotate, flip, set in plain blocks, just as you would on any other EQ4 layout style.

• To make sashing, set in plain blocks and stretch them to make sashes.

Setting Blocks into a Country Set Quilt

39

Rotating or Flipping Blocks

To rotate or flip a block in a quilt you must have a quilt on the screen.

Rotating Blocks

1   Click the Rotate tool.

2   Place your pointer (which looks like a rounded arrow) over a block on your quilt and click. The block rotates 90° every time you click.

Note: If you click too quickly, your click may not register.

3   Click Save in Sketchbook to save any new arrangement of blocks within a quilt.

Flipping Blocks

1   Click the Flip tool.

2   Place your cursor (which looks like a round arrow with a line through the middle) over a block on your quilt and click. The block will horizontally flip (from left to right).

3   Click Save in Sketchbook to save any new arrangement of blocks within a quilt.

 Notes & Tips ─────────────

• To rotate or flip every *other* block, hold down the ALT key and click. To rotate or flip *all* blocks, hold down the CTRL key and click.
• If your block is symmetrical (looks the same on each side) you will not be able to notice a rotation or flip.
• You can rotate a block other than 90° in a Country Set quilt.
• Rotate or Flip will work in any quilt layout or in any part of a quilt, including different layers and borders. However, you must be on the respective layer or border when you rotate or flip the block.

Step 1   *Your pointer will look like this, when you use the Rotate tool.*

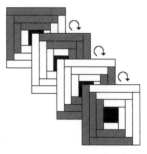

Step 2
Rotate your blocks as many times as you want until they look the way you want them to.

Step 1   *Your pointer will look like this, when you use the Flip tool.*

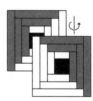

Step 2
Flipping gives you a mirror image of your original block.

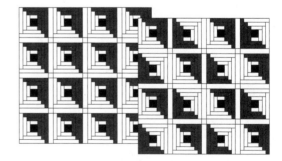

Log Cabins make diagonal stripes. This is just one example of what you can do using the Flip and Rotate tools.

Estimating Fabric Yardage

Step 2

Steps 3-5

EQ4 will estimate yardage for your quilt. Remember that these are estimates. You may find you need more or less fabric depending on how you cut out your pattern or whether you're using a special combination sewing/cutting method which has you trim fabric after sewing.

1   Have a quilt showing on the worktable.

Note:
If the quilt is in your Sketchbook, open the Sketchbook, click the Quilt tab, click the forward arrow to find the quilt, click the Edit button to get the quilt out of the Sketchbook.

2   On the FILE menu, point to Print, click Fabric yardage.

The Print Fabric Yardage box appears.

3   Select the fabric width and seam allowance settings that you want. EQ4 accounts for the fact that, for example, 45" fabric actually gives you about 42 usable inches.

4   Click the Preview button. A yardage chart appears.

5   Click the Print button to print the chart.

Notes & Tips

Here is how EQ4 figures yardage.

- It adds the seam allowance you select to each patch.
- It places an imaginary rectangle around each patch.
- It places these rectangles on fabric of the selected width.
- Each time a "row" is filled, it begins a new row, counting the entire strip as required yardage.

The result is generally an overestimate. Shapes like on-point sashes, for example, tend to give exceptionally large yardage figures. The estimate for the border generally requires a length of fabric as long as the longest border strip.

Backing and binding are not estimated.

Deleting a Quilt

Deleting a Saved Quilt from the Sketchbook

If you have saved a quilt in a project, or temporarily in the Sketchbook, you can delete it from the Sketchbook.

1 Click the View Sketchbook button.

2 Click the Quilts tab, if not already selected.

3 If you do not see the quilt you want to delete, click on the forward arrows until you do.

4 Click the Delete button. You will receive a message, "Delete this quilt. OK?"

5 Click Yes. The quilt will disappear from the Sketchbook.

6 Click the X in the bottom-right corner to close the Sketchbook.

7 Click the Save button to save your project if you have named and saved this project.

💡 **Notes & Tips**

- Deleting a quilt does not delete the individual blocks. The blocks will remain in your Sketchbook.
- To delete a block from a project and/or the Sketchbook, see: DELETING A BLOCK.

Step 1

Step 2

Step 3

Step 4

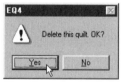
Step 5

Step 6

Step 7

Part 4
The Library

Part 4
The Library

Finding the Designer Fabrics

EQ4 has a wonderful library of scanned fabrics. These fabrics were generously supplied by top designers and manufacturers to give you the fun of trying out fabrics in the actual blocks you may be sewing.

To purchase these fabrics, ask for them at your local quilt or fabric store. Or see company Web sites for a store nearest you carrying that fabric.

When you use these fabrics, be aware that:

- All fabric in EQ4's Designer Fabric is copyrighted by the company that manufactures it.

- The actual fabric is more vibrant than the scanned image. This is particularly true with dark, or tone on tone prints.

- Scanned fabric uses a great deal of memory. This makes your projects large – something to consider in projects you intend to e-mail.

- Getting Designer Fabric automatically gives you coordinating solid colors. You'll see these solids in the Fabrics & Colors palette after you choose fabrics. Therefore, for a simple shortcut to get lovely solid colors: get a few print fabrics from the Designer Library.

- Most fabric prints are 50% of their actual size. The size of the fabric design will be the same in EQ4 whether used in a block or quilt.

- Any 256 color .bmp file can be used in EQ4. We suggest they do not exceed 200 X 200 pixels in size.

- You can add your own fabrics to the Fabric Library. See: ADDING FABRICS TO THE LIBRARY.

Finding the Designer Fabrics

Follow the steps below to find the Designer Fabrics.

1 On the LIBRARIES menu, click Fabric Library.

2 Double-click Designer Libraries. The list of designer libraries appears.

3 To use any fabrics in your designs see: GETTING FABRICS FROM THE LIBRARY.

Fabric Company Information

Balson-Erlanger

A Division of the Balson-Hercules Group Ltd.
1040 Avenue of the Americas
6th Floor
New York NY 10018
PHONE: 212-221-7100
FAX: 212-302-4386

Selection of floral prints and textures

Benartex Inc.

1460 Broadway
Eighth Floor
New York NY 10036
PHONE: 212-840-3250
FAX: 212-921-8204
E-MAIL: INFO@benartex.com
WEB SITE: http://www.benartex.com/zmain.html

Cumberland© by Marianne Fons and Liz Porter

Hermitage	Celia
Palmyra	Bluebell
Hickory	Briarwood
Julip	Westbury

Documentaries III©
Tamarind
Willow
Bamboo
Camellia

Fossil Fern© by Patricia B. Campbell

Impressions© by Pat Campbell and Michelle Jack

One-a-Day Prints©
Monday Washing Day
Tuesday Ironing Day
Wednesday Sewing Day
Thursday Visiting Day
Friday Sweeping Day
Saturday Baking Day
Sunday Church Day
Plaid
Polka Dots

Clothworks — A division of FASCO/Fabric Sales Co., Inc.

6250 Stanley Av, S.
Seattle, WA 98108
PHONE: 206-762-7886
FAX: 206-762-8809

Clothworks©
Staples© by Marsha McCloskey

Hoffman California Fabrics

25792 Obrero Drive
Mission Viejo CA 92691
PHONE: 949-770-2922
FAX: 949-770-4022
E-MAIL: hoffmanfab@aol.com
WEB SITE: http://hoffmanfabrics.com/

Coventry©
Les Jardins©
Petite Fleurs©
Windsor©

Kona Bay Fabrics

23 So. Vineyard Blvd.
Suite 305
Honolulu, HI 96813
PHONE: 808-533-1972
FAX: 808-533-1591
E-MAIL: konabay@pixi.com
WEB SITE: www.konabay.com

Best of Brittany & Rainbow Collections©
Taryn Collection©

Lunn Fabrics

Debra Lunn & Michael Mrowka
317 East Main Street
Lancaster, OH 43130-3845
PHONE: 740-654-2202
FAX: 740-654-3949
E-MAIL: redant@lunnfabrics.com
WEB SITE: http://www.lunnfabrics.com
Lunn Fabrics' tie dye fabrics, and others, can be purchased directly from Lunn Fabrics Web site.

Crystal Tie-Dye©
Strata Tie-Dye©

Moda Fabrics

United Notions & Fabrics
13795 Hutton Drive
Dallas TX 75234
PHONE: 972-484-8901
E-MAIL: moda@unitednotionsfabrics.com
WEB SITE: http://www.unitednotionsfabric.com

Brushed Plaids© by Linda Brannock and Jan Patek
English Oak©

Northcott/Monarch

229 West 36th Streeet
New York, NY10018
PHONE: 212-563-0450
E-MAIL: monarchcf@aol.com

Quilt For A Cure© fabrics in the **"Fine China Blue**©**"** collection designed by Bonnie Benn Stratton.
Note: A portion of the purchase price of every yard of Quilt For A Cure fabric is donated to The Breast Cancer Research Foundation. Fabrics are available in quilt shops and leading independent stores in the United States and Canada.
For more information contact:
Merryvale, Ltd., 11416 Vale Road, Oakton, VA 22124-1334; phone 703-264-8959.
For more information in Canada contact:
Northcott, 640 Rowntree Dairy Road, Woodbridge, ON L4L 5T8, Canada; phone 905-850-6675;
E-mail: northcot@ican.net

P & B Textiles

1580 Gilbreth Road
Burlingame, CA 94010
PHONE: 650-692-0422
FAX: 650-692-4908
E-MAIL: PandBTexSF@aol.com
WEB SITE: http://www.pbtex.com/home.html

Frostings© by Piece O' Cake Designs for P&B Textiles
Retro© by Gerald Roy (Pilgrim Roy) for P&B Textiles

Finding the Designer Fabrics

Robert Kaufman Co., Inc.

129 W 132ND St
Los Angeles CA 90061
PHONE: 310-538-3482
FAX: 310-538-9235

The Paisley Collection© by Jennifer Sampou

Rose & Hubble

1359 Broadway
9th Floor
New York NY 10018-2201
PHONE: 212-714-0999
FAX: 212-239-4008
E-MAIL: roseandhubble@erols.com

Flower Fairies©
Good Enough to Eat©

South Sea Imports

550 West Artesia Blvd.
Compton CA 90220
PHONE: 310-763-3800
FAX: 310-763-4777

Noah Charts His Course© by Debbie Mumm for South Sea Imports
Bunnies & Blooms© by Debbie Mumm for South Sea Imports
Roses, Rabbits & Other Fine Habits© by K.P. Kids for SSI

Westminster

Westminster Fibers, Inc.
5 Northern Blvd.
Suite 4
Amherst NH 03031-2335
PHONE: 603-886-5041
FAX: 603-886-1056
E-MAIL: wfibers@aol.com

Glorious Patchwork© prints by Kaffe Fassett

Finding the Designer Fabrics

Getting Blocks From the Library

The Block Library is full of quilt blocks. To use any blocks, you must "copy" them into your Sketchbook. Here is how to find the blocks and get any of them into your Sketchbook.

Step 1

1   On the LIBRARIES menu, click Block Library. You will see a "book" named EQ Libraries. These are the EQ4 blocks.

2   Double-click one of the books. A list of secondary books will appear.

3   Double-click one of the secondary books. Pages will pop-up.

4   Double-click a page. Blocks from that page will appear.

Step 2

Tip:

Look above the blocks to see the name of the secondary book and page where the blocks are from. Hold your cursor over a block (don't click), to make the block's name appear.

5   Click any block to select it. A white frame will surround the block.

Step 3

6   Click Copy. The block will "disappear" to show it has been taken from the Library and put into your Sketchbook. You can get as many blocks as you want. They can be from different books and pages.

7   Click Close to put the Block Library away.

💡 **Notes & Tips** ─────────

•   You can view either 4, 9, or 16 blocks on the screen at a time. At the center bottom of the Block Libraries menu there are 3 buttons; one has 4 squares, one with 9, and the third with 16 tiny squares. Click the button that has the number of squares you want to be on your screen. The fewer blocks that are on the screen the bigger and more detailed they will appear.

•   You can view the blocks in 3 colorways: line drawing (no coloring), grayscale, or multicolor. You may change the view style by clicking on the coloring arrows. When you take a block from the library you automatically get it in all 3 colorways.

Step 4

Getting Blocks from the Library

Step 6

- You cannot "use up" the library blocks. They will always remain in the library, ready to be used no matter how often you copy a block.
- You can draw your own blocks and add them to the library. See: SAVING BLOCKS IN THE LIBRARY
- To retrieve/use/color your library blocks, see: GETTING BLOCKS FROM THE SKETCHBOOK.
- If you see "strange" colors in the blocks *you* saved in the library, it's because you saved blocks colored with fabric prints. EQ4 changes the print to a solid.

Now you can see the blocks you selected in your Sketchbook.

Getting Fabrics from the Library

The Fabric Library has thousands of fabrics. Some are computer-drawn fabrics. Others are real scanned fabrics. Follow the steps below to find the fabrics and use any swatches you like.

1   On the LIBRARIES menu, click Fabric Library. You will see different books in the library (EQ Libraries, My Libraries, and Designer Libraries).

Step 1

Note:
EQ Libraries are computer drawings of fabric. My Libraries are empty spaces, waiting to hold your own scanned fabric. Designer Libraries are full of pre-scanned "real" fabrics.

2   Double-click one of these books and you will see more books.

Step 2

Step 3

3   Double-click one of the secondary books and you will see pages of specific fabric groups.

4   Double-click one of the pages and you will instantly see fabric swatches from that page, or collection, pop up on the right side of the screen.

Note:
You can either view 4, 9, or 16 fabric swatches at a time. At the center-bottom of the Fabric Libraries menu there are 3 buttons; one with 4 squares, one with 9, and the third with 16. Click on the button showing the number of swatches you want to view. The fewer fabric patches on the screen, the bigger and more detailed they will appear.

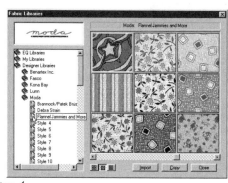

Step 4
These are just a few of the thousands of fabrics available in EQ4.

5   Click a fabric swatch (a white frame will surround it).

6   Click Copy. The fabric will "disappear" which means it has been sent to the Sketchbook and will be ready to use when you color.

7   Click on as many fabrics as you want and copy them. You can open other books and pages and copy fabrics.

8   When you are done copying fabrics, click

Step 9

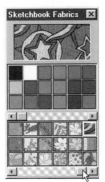

Step 10

Close. You will be back at your block or quilt layout. You will see a progress bar, indicating that fabrics are being loaded.

9 Click on the Paintbrush tool.

10 Click, hold, and drag the slider under the pattern swatches to the end (right) of the palette and you will see your copied fabrics. You will also find new coordinating solid colors.

11 Now, you can click on any of the new fabric swatches and color your blocks and quilts. Have fun with the thousands of fabrics!

Note:

Once you exit EQ4, the fabrics you copied out of the Fabric Library will go back into the library. When you open EQ4 again, you can copy new fabrics from the Fabric Library.

To save a group of fabrics permanently, save them in a project file by saving a project.

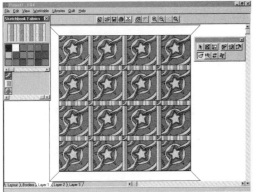

A finished quilt with designer fabrics!

Getting Fabrics from the Library

Saving Fabrics in the Library

Have you made some nifty new print fabric colorways or scanned some of your own fabrics? Then save them in the Fabric Library (as well as in a project). Saving fabrics in the Fabric Library is the only way to make them available so you do not have to repeat the new colorways or scanning steps.

1   If you have created a new colorway for a print fabric, or have scanned, imported, and copied fabric, it will be in the Sketchbook. (It has to be in order to save it to the library.)

2   On the LIBRARIES menu, click Add Fabrics. You will see a User Libraries book with Library books under it.

3   Click the + sign by the first Library book. Style pages will appear. These pages are empty, waiting for you to fill them with fabrics.

4   Click any style page symbol to select that style. The "Current Style" window will say "No Fabrics" unless you have previously added fabrics to this style.

5   In the window above Fabric Sketchbook, click on the fabric patch you want to add to the library. This puts a white frame around the patch. (If you do not see your fabric, click, hold, and drag the slider bar under the Sketchbook to view all of the patches.)

6   Click Copy. You will now see your fabric patch under Current Style.

Note
> The fabric will still appear in the Fabric Sketchbook. But if you try to copy the fabric again, the program will not allow it. You will receive a message reading, "This fabric is already in the current library style!"

7   Click Save Library. A message saying, "Your fabrics have been saved in the library!" will appear.

You must save the library before you close

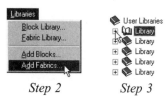

Step 2   *Step 3*

Step 4

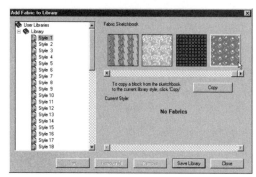

Step 5

Step 6

Step 7

Step 8

Step 1

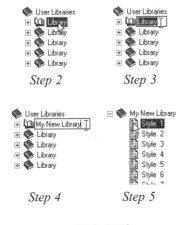

Step 2   *Step 3*

Step 4   *Step 5*

Step 6

Step 7

it or else the new fabric(s) will not be saved.

8 You may copy as many fabrics as you want. Click Close when you have finished adding fabrics.

Renaming Your Library

1 On the LIBRARIES menu, click Add Fabrics.

2 Click once on the library you want to rename. The name will become high-lighted (darkened).

3 Click on the word again. A box will form around it.

4 Type your new name (up to 32 characters long). The old name will disappear as you type.

5 Click on the style you saved your new fabric in, so you can see it displayed.

   You do not have to rename the style (although you can if you want), but it does have to be visible to save the changes to the Library.

6 Click Save Library. A message saying, "Your fabrics have been saved in the library!" will appear. You've saved your new library name.

7 Click Close when you are finished renaming.

💡 **Notes & Tips** ─────────────

- **You can make any print fabric (from the library or scanned) in new colorways. See:** MAKING PRINT FABRIC IN NEW COLORWAYS.

- **Scan fabrics. See:** IMPORTING SCANNED FABRICS.

- **To remove a fabric patch from the style, click the patch you want to remove, then click Remove. The program will ask, "Remove the selected fabric from the current library style. OK?" Click Yes if this is the fabric you want to remove. (Click No if it is not.) To remove *all* fabric patches from a style, click Remove All. Remember to save the library after any changes.**

Saving Fabrics in the Library

55

Saving Blocks in the Library

Do you draw your own blocks? Want them handy to use in *any* project? Then save them in the Block Library (as well as in a project). Saving blocks in the Block Library is the only way to make them available so you can combine blocks from different projects. Don't try saving blocks colored with print fabrics in the library. (You *can* save print-colored blocks in projects.) Fabric prints won't be saved with the block in the library, but the drawing will (you'll just see solids). To use your saved library blocks in any project, get them from the library and recolor them, using whatever prints or solids you choose.

1 When you have a block on the screen, and want to save it in the Block Library, you need to save it to the Sketchbook first, so click the Save in Sketchbook button.

2 On the LIBRARIES menu, click Add Blocks. You will see a User Libraries book with Library books under it.

3 Click the + sign by the first Library book. Style pages will appear. These pages are empty, waiting for you to fill them with blocks.

4 Click any style page symbol to select that style. The "Current Style" window will say "No Blocks" unless you have previously added blocks to this style.

5 In the window above Block Sketchbook, click on the block you want to add to the library. This puts a white frame around the block. (If you do not see your block, click, hold, and drag the slider bar under the Sketchbook to view all of the blocks.)

6 Click Copy. You will now see your block under Current Style.

Note:
The block will still appear in the Block Sketchbook. But if you try to copy the block again, the program will not allow it. You will receive a message reading, "This block is

Step 1

Step 2

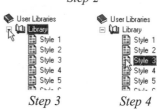

Step 3   *Step 4*

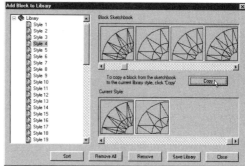

Step 6

We've clicked on Copy several times, to show that you can select as many blocks as you wish.

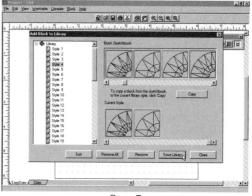

Step 7

already in the current library style!"

7   Click Save Library. A message saying, "Your blocks have been saved in the library!" will appear.

You must save the library before you close it or else the new block(s) will not be saved.

Step 8

8   Click Close when you have finished adding blocks.

Renaming Your Library

1   On the LIBRARIES menu, click Add Block.

2   Click once on the library you want to rename. (Or open a library, and click once on the style name you want to rename.) The name will become highlighted (darkened).

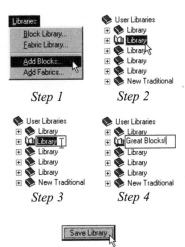

Step 1   *Step 2*

Step 3   *Step 4*

Step 5

Step 6

3   Click on the word again. A box will form around it.

4   Type your new name (up to 32 characters long). The old name will disappear as you type.

5   Click Save Library. A message saying, "Your blocks have been saved in the library!" will appear. You've saved your new library name.

6   Click Close when you are finished renaming.

💡 **Notes & Tips** ─────────────

•   **Remember, if you save blocks colored with print fabrics in the library, you will save the blocks, not the fabrics. When you get the blocks from the library, just recolor the blocks.**

•   **To remove a block from the style, click the block you want to remove, then click Remove. The program will ask, "Remove the selected block from the current library style. OK?" Click Yes if this is the block you want to remove. (Click No if it is not.) To remove *all* blocks from a style, click Remove All. Remember to save the library after any changes.**

Saving Blocks in the Library

Part 5
Blocks

Part 5
Blocks

Drawing a Grid

Step 1

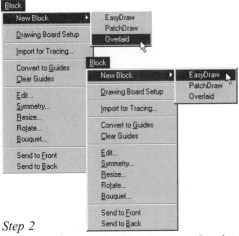

Step 2

You can choose either EasyDraw or Overlaid.

Step 3

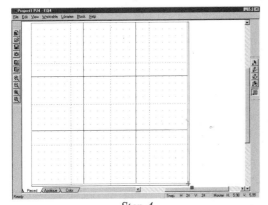

Step 4

Clicking on the little black square brings up the Grid Properties menu.

The grid tool lets you make instant 4-patch, 9-patch, and so on up to 144-patch blocks, great for watercolor grids.

1 On the WORKTABLE menu, click Work on Block.

2 On the BLOCK menu, point to New Block, click either EasyDraw or Overlaid. (For a pieced block, choose EasyDraw. For a combination pieced and applique block, choose Overlaid.)

3 Click the Grid tool.

4 Point the mouse cursor to line up the crosshair at the block's top-left corner. Click, hold, and drag the mouse diagonally down and across your block, to the opposite corner. A grid forms as you draw. Release the mouse when the grid fills your block.

Changing the grid's patch number

To change your grid's patch number, you must click *carefully* on the grid tool's black square.

1 Select the Grid tool by clicking the little black square in the Grid tool's bottom-left corner. The Grid Properties pop–up appears.

2 Click on the left and right arrow keys to change the number of columns and rows. Values can range from 2 to 12.

Notes & Tips

• **Make sure the number of grid divisions divides evenly into the number of snap to points. For example, don't draw a 5 x 5 patch grid if you have 24 x 24 snap to points. 24 can't be evenly divided by 5. Instead, increase the snap to points to 25 x 25 (on the BLOCK menu, choose Drawing Board Setup), then draw your 5 x 5 patch.**

Drawing a Grid

Making Drawing Guides

You can make guidelines to help you as you draw blocks. Making a 4-Patch grid, for example, and changing it to guides helps you find your block's center. Guides will not appear in your final block design.

1   On the WORKTABLE menu, click Work on Block.

2   On the BLOCK menu, point to New Block, click on EasyDraw, PatchDraw, or Overlaid.

3   Draw anything you would like to use as guides.

4   *Right*-click anywhere on the screen. A pop-up menu will appear.

5   Click on Convert to Guides. The solid lines change to colored, dotted lines. These are guides. You can look at the guides as you draw.

Clear Guides

To clear guides from your drawing screen, choose Clear Guides.

1   *Right*-click anywhere on the screen. A pop-up menu will appear.

2   Click on Clear Guides. All of your guides will be erased or cleared. There is no way to clear one line at a time.

💡 **Notes & Tips** —————————

- **To change the color of the guides, click on the BLOCK menu and click on Drawing Board Setup. On the General tab, in the Color box, click on the down arrow under Guides. Click on one of the eight colors that pops up. Click OK. The guides will change to the newly selected color.**
- **You can change any block or grid to guides.**

Step 1

Step 2
You can choose PatchDraw or Overlaid, but for our example, we're using EasyDraw.

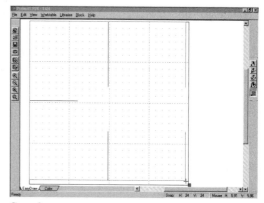

Step 3
You can draw anything you like to use as a guide, but for our example, we're using the Grid tool.

Step 5

- To change some block lines or patches to guides, leaving others as "real" lines, click the Select tool, and hold down the SHIFT key while you click on any lines or patches you want to change to guides. Then right-click to pop-up the menu, and choose Convert to Guides. Only the selected lines will change to guides.

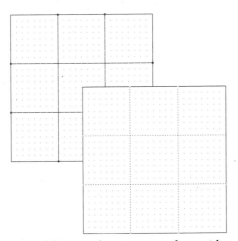

The grid has now been converted to guides.

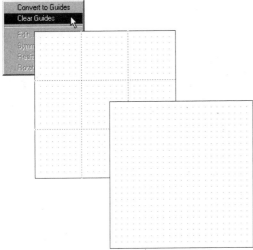

Clear Guides will remove ALL guides from your block.

Making Drawing Guides

Making Graph Paper

You can make graph paper-like guidelines show up on your block to help you draw. These lines will not appear when you color, print, or use the block in a quilt. You can use graph paper in any of the three block layouts (EasyDraw, PatchDraw, or Overlaid).

1   On the WORKTABLE menu, click Work on Block.

2   On the BLOCK menu, click Drawing Board Setup.

3   On the Drawing Board Setup pop-up menu, click the Graph Paper tab.

4   Click the up and down arrows to select Number of Divisions from 2 to 48 units for both horizontal and vertical. (If you choose 2 for both Horizontal and Vertical you will have 4 squares. If you choose 48 for both you will have 2304 squares – whew, sounds challenging!)

5   Under Options, you can select the color of the graph paper. Click the down arrow (beside Graph paper color), click one of the eight colors, then click OK. The graph paper lines will change to the newly selected color.

6   For Style there are two options: to have graph paper or not. Click the down arrow (beside Style), click Graph paper lines to show the graph (or Blank to not have graph lines). Click OK, the graph paper lines will appear on your block.

Step 1

Step 2

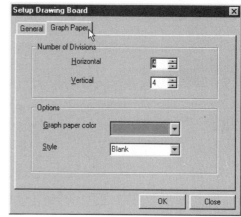

Step 3

 Notes & Tips ───────────

•   **When determining how many divisions to make – look at your block's Snap to number. Make sure the number of divisions divides evenly into the number of snap points. For example, if your block has 24 x 24 snap points – make your number of graph paper divisions 2,3,4,6,8 etc. rather than 5 or 7.**

Eliminating the PatchDraw Background

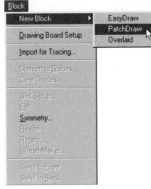

Step 1

Step 2

PatchDraw blocks automatically have backgrounds. For example, the background for a Sunbonnet Sue block is the background fabric square Sue is on. If you do not want a background square, you can get rid of it. You may want to eliminate the background in order to "float" applique patches in Layer 2 of your quilt.

1   On the WORKTABLE menu, click Work on Block.

2   On the BLOCK menu, point to New Block, click on PatchDraw.

3   Click on the Select tool.

4   Click on the square which makes up the background/outline of the block (Nodes will surround the square.)

5   Press the DELETE key on your keyboard. The background will disappear. Isn't that easy!

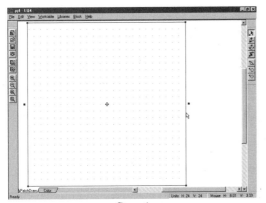

Step 4

💡 **Notes & Tips**

• If you decide you want the background to reappear you can: click on the EDIT menu and click Undo Clear (if you decide immediately after you delete the background); click on the BLOCK menu, point to New Block, and click on PatchDraw (if you're not worried about saving the block).

• You can draw your own background square, but be aware it may not be the exact outline of the block. Therefore, it is easier to use the default background.

• If you draw a background after other patches are made, you must send the background to the back when you color the block. See:
   LAYERING PATCHES.

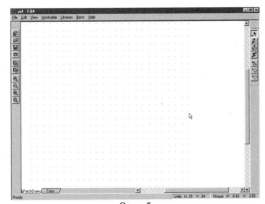

Step 5

Drawing a Rectangular Block

To draw a rectangular block you first change the shape of the block outline.

1 On the WORKTABLE menu, click Work on Block.

Step 1

2 On the BLOCK menu, point to New Block, click EasyDraw, PatchDraw, or Overlaid.

3 On the BLOCK menu, click Drawing Board Setup. The Drawing Board Setup box will appear with the General tab selected.

4 Under block size, change the Horizontal and Vertical sizes to the rectangular size you want. To change the size, click before the number and drag your cursor over the number. Release the mouse and the number will be highlighted.

5 Type a number between 1 and 48 for the horizontal and the vertical size of the block.

Note:
Press your keyboard TAB key and your cursor will automatically jump to the Vertical block size, highlighting the current number.

6 Click OK. The block size will change on the worktable.

Step 2
For our example we'll be using EasyDraw.

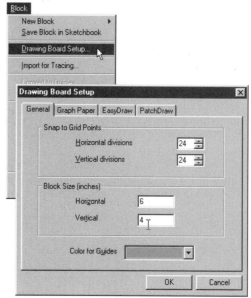

Steps 3-5

💡 **Notes & Tips** ─────────

• Your rectangular block will show up as a square block in the Sketchbook and in the Sketchbook Blocks box, when you are ready to set the block into a quilt. Don't worry. If you print the block, or set it into a rectangular block, sash or border space, it will be rectangular and look proportioned just as you have drawn it.

Step 6

Drawing a Rectangular Block

Coloring a Block

Step 1

Step 2

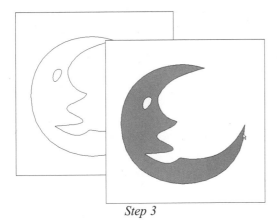

Step 3

Once you're finished designing a block you can color it. You can be in an EasyDraw, PatchDraw, or Overlaid layout to color.

1   Click on the Color tab at the bottom of the block layout. Your drawing will appear, the Paintbrush tool will be selected, and the Fabrics & Colors palette will pop up.

2   Click on a fabric (patterned) or a color (solid) swatch.

3   Click on a patch in your block and watch it change to your selected color. Coloring is that easy!

💡 **Notes & Tips** ─────────

- Use the slider bars and arrows underneath both the Color and Fabric swatches to view all of the colors in the palette.
- You can go back and forth from the block-layout screen to the color screen, but be sure and save your drawing each time a change is made.
- Your block drawing appears much clearer on the Color tab/screen because all of the nodes are hidden. Flipping between the block layout (EasyDraw, PatchDraw, or Overlaid) and color tabs is a good way to see how a drawing is progressing.
- If you do not see one of your patches when you click on the Color tab, don't worry. If you drew a larger patch over a smaller patch the smaller patch will not appear. You will need to send the larger patch to the back in order to see the smaller patch (see: LAYERING PATCHES).
- If you colored multiple patches the same color and want to change that color see: RECOLORING MULTIPLE PATCHES.
- If you want other fabrics to color with see: GETTING FABRICS FROM THE LIBRARY.
- If you want other solid colors to color with see: CREATING NEW COLORS.
- You can color blocks copied from the library. From the Sketchbook, click on the block you want to color and click Edit. The line drawing of the block will appear. Color as if it were your own design.

Recoloring Multiple Patches

The Spraycan and Swap tools are used for recoloring multiple patches instantly. To change all red patches to blue, for example, you would use the Spraycan to recolor one block; the Swap tool to recolor the whole quilt.

Using the Spraycan tool:

1   Click the Spraycan tool. The Fabrics & Colors palette will pop up.

2   Click on any patch in any colored block. (This can include blocks in sashes, corner blocks, and borders.) This selects (dashed lines surround) every patch with the same color.

3   Click any color or fabric swatch in the palette. This "spray" paints the selected patches instantly.

Tip:
Changing colors instantly in alternate blocks in any quilt:

With the Spraycan tool (or Swap tool) selected, hold down the ALT key and click on any block patch.

Using the Swap tool:

1   Click the Swap tool. The Fabrics & Colors palette will pop up.

2   Click on any patch in any colored block on your quilt. (This can include blocks in sashes, corner blocks, and borders.) This selects every similarly colored patch.

3   Click any color or fabric swatch in the palette. This "swaps" colors in all selected patches instantly.

Note:
You can also swap colors, with the Spraycan tool selected, by holding down the CTRL key and clicking on any block patch.

Step 1

Step 2

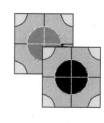

Step 3

Step 1

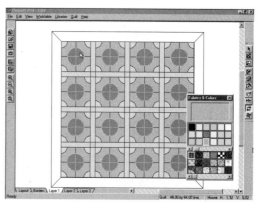

Step 2

Recoloring Multiple Patches

Layering Patches

Step 1

Step 2

Step 4

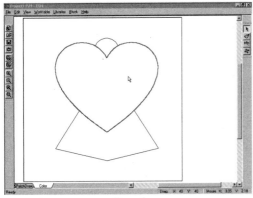

Step 6

Step 7

The angel's wings are where they should be.

When patches overlap you'll sometimes want to move a patch in front of, or behind another patch. Once your block is drawn, to move patches "to front" or "to back" you will need to click on the Color tab. You will be looking at your black and white line drawing.

1   On the WORKTABLE menu, click Work on Block.

2   On the BLOCK menu, point to New Block, choose PatchDraw or Overlaid. (Then click the Appliqué tab for Overlaid.)

3   Draw your block. Once your block is drawn, you can move patches in front of ("to front") or behind ("to back") other patches.

4   Click the Color tab at screen bottom.

5   Click the Select tool.

6   Click a patch you want to move. A colored frame will surround the patch.

7   *Right*-click anywhere on the screen. A pop-up menu will appear.

8   Click Send to Front and the patch will be the top layer or Send to Back so the patch will be the bottom layer.

Notes & Tips

- Patches that overlap are automatically layered in the order they are drawn. The last patch drawn, for example, will automatically be on top.
- You can change the layering before or after you've colored patches.
- If you change a layer and you don't like the new look, you can "Undo" the most recent change. Click the EDIT menu and click "Undo..."

Layering Patches

69

Combining Pieced and Applique Blocks

You can use applique motifs in pieced blocks. We'll start with two library blocks, then "float" some applique flowers on the pieced design.

1 On the WORKTABLE menu, click Work on Block.

2 Select and copy both a pieced and an applique motif block from the library to the Sketchbook. Then close the Block Library.

See: GETTING BLOCKS FROM THE LIBRARY.

Note:
For this recipe we used these two blocks:

Pieced block: 2 Contemporary Pieced / Country Houses / Picket Fence

Applique block: 6 Applique Motifs / Simple Designs / the sun design

3 Click the View Sketchbook button. The Sketchbook will appear.

4 Click the Block tab. The library blocks you copied will appear.

5 Click the pieced block. A frame will surround the block.

6 Click the Edit button. The Sketchbook will close and the block will appear on the EasyDraw worktable.

7 On the EDIT menu, click Select All. The lines of the pieced block will be highlighted (darkened).

8 On the EDIT menu, click Copy. You will not see anything happen. But the block has been copied to the clipboard.

9 On the BLOCK menu, point to New Block, click Overlaid. The Overlaid block worktable will appear. It will be blank.

10 Click the Pieced tab, if it is not already selected.

11 On the EDIT menu, click Paste. Your pieced block will appear.

Step 1

Step 3

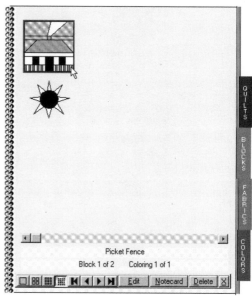

Step 5

Step 6

Step 7

Step 8

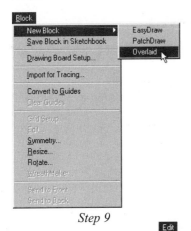

Step 9

Step 10

Step 11

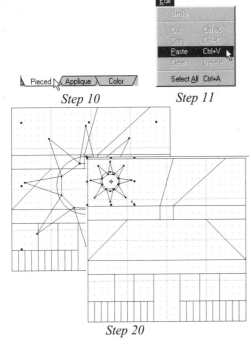

Step 20

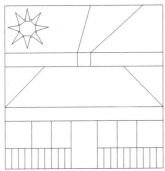

The finished block

12 While the block is still highlighted, click hold, and drag the block to make it "snap" into place perfectly on the block outline.

Note:
If necessary, you can select (highlight) the block again in order to move it. On the EDIT menu, click Select All, to highlight the block. Then drag the block.

13 Click the Save in Sketchbook button so your block is saved. (You'll use it later.)

14 Repeat steps 3 - 8 for the applique block.

15 Click the View Sketchbook button.

16 On the Block tab, click the Overlaid block you just saved.

17 Click the Edit button. The Overlaid block will appear.

18 Click the Applique tab. You will still see the pieced block.

19 On the EDIT menu, click Paste. Your applique will appear on the pieced block. You may want to move it. While it is still highlighted, click, hold, and drag the applique patch to move it.

20 To resize it, while it is still highlighted, point to a corner node, and drag the node to make the applique smaller.

Or see: RESIZING A BLOCK PATCH.

21 Click the Save in Sketchbook button.

At this point your block is done and you can color it or set it into a quilt.

See:

SETTING BLOCKS INTO A QUILT LAYOUT

COLORING BLOCKS IN A QUILT

ROTATING OR FLIPPING A DRAWING

Combining Pieced and Applique Blocks

Rotating or Flipping a Drawing

If you have a Block Drawing on the WORK-TABLE, you may want to flip all or part of your drawing.

Rotating by Degrees

This method shows you how to rotate by 90, 180 or 270 degrees. It is recommended for EasyDraw, PatchDraw and Overlaid blocks.

1   Click the Select tool.

2   Click the line or patch you want to rotate or flip. Selected lines or patches will appear highlighted (darker in EasyDraw, surrounded by nodes in PatchDraw).

Note:
> To select more than one line, hold down the SHIFT **key as you click.**

3   On the Select tool, click the small black square at the bottom left. The Symmetry pop-up menu will appear. You will see 8 different buttons, specifically 3 Rotate ("Rot") buttons, 4 Flip buttons, and Clone.

Using the Symmetry pop-up menu you can rotate by 90, 180, or 270 degrees. You can also flip horizontally (H), vertically (V), down (D), or over (O).

4   Click one of the rotate or flip buttons to see how it changes your drawing.

Rotating by using the mouse

This method is recommended for PatchDraw blocks *only*.

1   Click the Select tool.

2   Click a patch and it will appear highlighted (darker) with eight small boxes (nodes) around it.

3   Holding down the CTRL key, click the center icon which looks like two crossed double-sided arrows. The center icon will now look like a bull's eye and the sur-

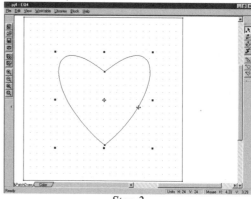

Step 2

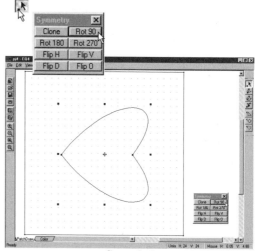

Steps 3-4

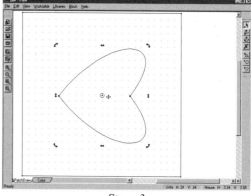

Steps 3

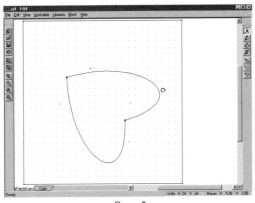

Step 5

rounding nodes will be double-sided arrows.

4   Move the cursor over one of the curved, *corner* arrows until it changes into the rotate cursor. (If you don't choose the corner arrow, your patch will pivot rather than rotate.)

5   Click, hold, and drag the mouse in the desired direction to rotate, releasing the mouse when the select is at the desired angle.

6   To get out of the mouse-rotate mode, click outside of the highlighted patch.

💡 **Notes & Tips** ───────────────

- **When rotating by specific degree, you can rotate or flip multiple parts of your drawing at once. Click SHIFT + the drawing to select/ highlight multiple parts.**
- **To rotate by a specific degree, on the BLOCK menu, click on Rotate. Type in the specific degree or drag the slider bar to the angle you would like to rotate your drawing. You can rotate between 1 and 359 degrees.**
- **To rotate or flip entire blocks in quilt layouts, see: ROTATING OR FLIPPING BLOCKS.**
- **Using the mouse to rotate makes it difficult to return to the original orientation of the drawing, so make sure that you really want to rotate or that precision is not important. If not, select Undo from the Edit menu before proceeding.**

Rotating or Flipping a Drawing

Resizing a Block Patch

At any point while you're drawing a block, you can resize one or many patches. You can be working on an EasyDraw, PatchDraw, or Overlaid block.

1   Have your block on the worktable, then click the Select tool.

2   Click the block line or patch you want to resize. Selected lines or patches will appear highlighted (surrounded by nodes in PatchDraw).

3   On the BLOCK menu, click Resize. The Resize pop-up box will appear.

4   Click, hold, and drag the slider bar to the percentage you want to increase or decrease your patch by when it resizes.

5   Click OK. Your patch will automatically change size.

Step 1

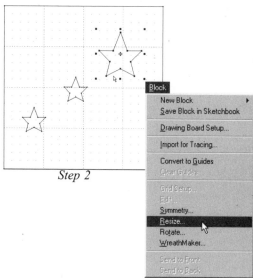

Step 2

Step 3

💡 **Notes & Tips** ───────────

• To resize multiple lines or patches, hold down the SHIFT key while clicking on the segments.
• If you cannot get the slider bar to stop exactly on the percent you want, don't worry. You can manually type in any number. Place your cursor in front of the number and click the mouse button. Hold down the mouse button, click and drag the cursor over the number. Type the number you want. Click OK to see the new block size appear.
• Resizing values range from 10 to 300 percent.
• Make sure the new patch size does not extend past the block border. You may have to move the newly sized patch.
• If you want to rotate or flip the newly resized patch, see ROTATING OR FLIPPING A DRAWING.
• To resize the entire block, choose Select All on the EDIT menu.
• To erase the new patch, choose "Undo resize select" from the EDIT menu immediately after resizing.
• To reduce the size of the entire block to a quarter patch, see: SHRINKING A BLOCK TO A QUARTER PATCH.

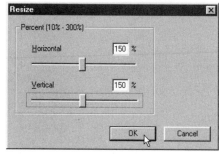

Steps 4-5

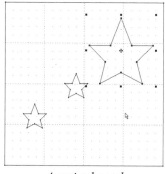

A resized patch

Copying Lines or Patches

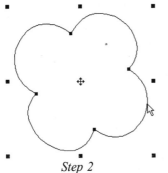

Step 2

Clicking on this patch selects the whole patch

Step 3

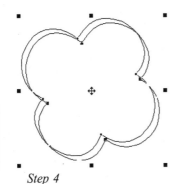

Step 4

You can be working on an EasyDraw, PatchDraw, or Overlaid block to copy any part of your drawing.

1   Click the Select tool.

2   Click the segment you want to copy. It will appear highlighted (darker in EasyDraw. To copy more than one line or patch, hold down the SHIFT key while clicking on lines or patches you want to copy).

3   On the Select tool, click the small black square at the bottom-left. The Symmetry pop-up menu will appear. You will see 8 different buttons, specifically 3 Rotate ("Rot") buttons, 4 Flip buttons, and Clone.

4   Click Clone. The copy will be slightly offset to the lower-right of the original. To move the copy–click, hold and drag the copy to a new spot on your block.

5   Click Clone again to make another copy.

Notes & Tips

- When the copied segment appears it will be highlighted (selected) making it easier to move or further alter (rotate or flip) at that time.
- On the EDIT menu, you can also click on Copy and then Paste to achieve the same result as Clone.

Making New Blocks from Old Blocks

You can invent new block designs by making changes to any block you find in EQ4. To do this you get a block from the Block Library, then erase or add lines to change it, and save it as a new block.

Step 1

1   On the LIBRARIES menu, click Block Library.

2   Get a block from the library.

    For help getting a block from the library into your Sketchbook see: GETTING BLOCKS FROM THE LIBRARY.

3   Click the View Sketchbook button.

Step 3

    The Sketchbook opens, and you will see the block you got out of the library.

4   Click your block, to select it.

5   Click the Edit button.

    The block is now on the block worktable with the tools you need for editing.

Note:
If you want to get a block from a project you've made, open the project, find the block in the Sketchbook, click the block to select it, click the Edit button.

Adding or Deleting Lines

6   To draw more lines on the block, click the Line tool to turn the cursor into a drawing cursor. Draw lines on the block.

7   To delete a line, click the Select tool, click the line you want to delete. Press your keyboard DELETE key.

8   To delete an entire patch, click the Select tool, point to the top-left of the patch, drag your mouse to the right and down. A select box forms as you drag. When you release the mouse, everything inside the select box will be selected. Press your keyboard DELETE key.

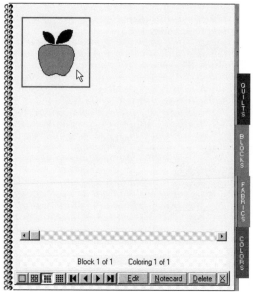

Step 4

Step 5

We edited the original apple block to look like an eaten apple. There is no limit to how you can modify EQ4's existing blocks to make your own!

Converting Block Lines to Guides

You can draw a new block while looking at another block. Do this by first changing all or any lines into guides — dotted lines visible only as you draw; invisible when you color.

9   Point the mouse pointer at the block drawing on the worktable and RIGHT-click. A menu appears.

10   Click Convert to Guides. Your block lines will change to dotted guides.

Note:
   To change *some* lines to guides, leaving others, click the Select tool, select the lines, right-click on the block, click Convert to Guides. Only the selected lines will change into guides.

 Notes & Tips ──────────

• Be sure to click Save in Sketchbook to save your new block drawing.

• You can save your new block in the block library. **See:** SAVING BLOCKS IN THE BLOCK LIBRARY.

Shrinking a Block to a Quarter Patch

Once you have a block on your screen, you can shrink it to make it part of a new design. You can be working on an EasyDraw, PatchDraw, or Overlaid block to resize.

1 On the EDIT menu, click Select All. The entire block will be highlighted (appear darker) and surrounded by nodes.

2 On the BLOCK menu, click Resize. The Resize pop-up menu will appear.

3 Click, hold, and drag the slider bar to 50 for both Horizontal and Vertical.

Note:
If you cannot get the slider bar to stop exactly on 50, you can manually type in any number. Place your cursor in front of the number in the Horizontal field and click the mouse button (the cursor will be flashing). Hold down the mouse button, click and drag the cursor over the number (the number will appear highlighted). Type the number you want (as soon as you start typing the original/highlighted number will disappear). Press the Tab key on your keyboard twice, and it will take you down to theVertical field automatically highlighting the number for you, so that all you have to do is type in the number.

4 Click OK. Your block will automatically appear smaller.

5 While the block is still selected, click, hold, and drag it to the top-left corner. Make sure the top-left corner of the smaller block is lined up as closely as possible with the top-left corner of the block outline.

6 Release the mouse and the smaller block will automatically "snap" to the top-left corner of the block outline.
While the shrunken block is still highlighted, you can make copies of it (see: COPYING PATCHES or follow these shortcut steps: Click EDIT – Copy – EDIT – Paste – drag to a corner – EDIT – Paste – drag to a corner) and place them in the other corners of the block.

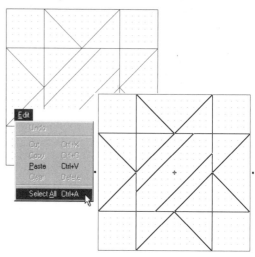

Step 1 –
this shows the Variable Star block selected

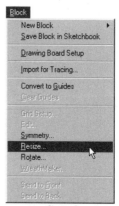

Step 2

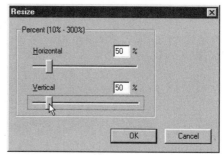

Step 3

Shrinking a Block to a Quarter Patch

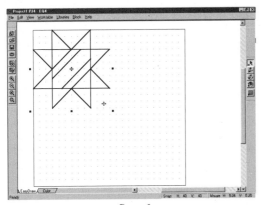

Step 6

Optional: You can draw a 2x2 grid in your block to complete the block. (See: DRAWING A GRID.)

Notes & Tips

Values for resizing by degree range from 10 to 300.

- When resizing an Overlaid block, you must resize the Pieced and Applique layers separately.
- You can also resize selected segments by dragging a node with the mouse.
- You can resize different blocks and combine them in a block outline. Shrink the first block, place it in the block outline, and save it. Then shrink another block, clone it (see: COPYING PATCHES), open up the saved block, and set (paste) the clone into the block outline.

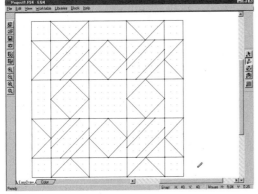

The finished block made by shrinking and repeating a Variable Star – uncolored

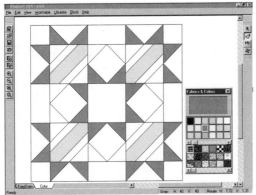

The finished block with color–
The way you color a block like this changes the way it looks dramatically.

Shrinking a Block to a Quarter Patch

Deleting a Block

Delete a Saved Block from the Library

You can delete blocks *you* save in the LIBRARY. (You cannot delete EQ4's library blocks.)

1   On the LIBRARIES menu, click Add Blocks. You will see a User Library book with 5 Library books under it.

2   Click the + sign beside the Library book containing the block you want to delete.

3   Click the style containing the block you want to delete.

4   Click the block you want to delete. (If you don't see your block, click, hold, and drag the slider bar to view all blocks.)

5   Click the Remove button. You will receive a message asking, "Remove the selected block from the current library style. OK?"

6   Click Yes. The block will disappear.

7   Click the Save Library button. You will receive a message saying, "Your blocks have been saved in the library!"

8   Click OK. The change will be made permanently.

9   Click the Close button. The library will close. You will be back at your worktable.

Delete a Block from a Project

You can delete a block you have saved in a project. To do so you must open the project, delete the block, then resave your project. (If the block is only in your Sketchbook, not yet saved in a project, just follow steps 4 - 9 below.)

1   On the FILE menu, click Open.

2   On the Open an Existing Project tab, click on the project you want to open, to highlight the project name.

3   Click OK.

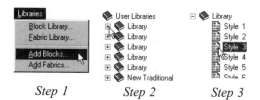

Step 1   *Step 2*   *Step 3*

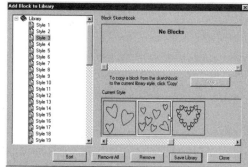

Step 4

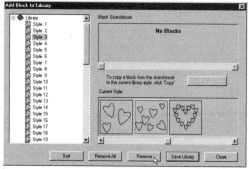

Step 5

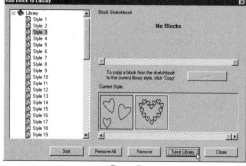

Step 7

Deleting a Block

Step 1

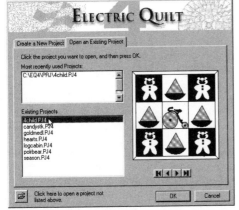

Step 2

4 Click the View Sketchbook button.

5 Click the Blocks tab.

6 Click the block you want to delete. (If you don't see your block, click, hold, and drag the slider bar to view all blocks.)

7 Click the colorings arrows to view the block as a black and white line drawing.

8 Click the Delete button. You will receive a message, "Delete this block and all its colors. OK?"

9 Click Yes. The block will disappear from the Sketchbook.

10 Click the Save button. You must resave your changed project, to make a permanent change.

💡 **Notes & Tips**

- **To delete only a specific coloring of the block, not the block itself, have that coloring appearing when you click Delete. You will receive the message, "Delete this coloring. OK?" Click Yes.**
- **To delete a quilt from a project and/or the Sketchbook, see:** DELETING A QUILT.
- **If you delete a block used in quilts, you will receive a message asking, "This coloring is used in a quilt! Delete Anyway?" If you click Yes to delete the block, the block will also be deleted from quilts.**

Step 5

Step 6

Step 7

Step 8

Deleting a Block

81

Deleting Lines or Patches

You can be working on an EasyDraw, PatchDraw, or Overlaid block to delete any part of your drawing.

1 Click on the Select tool.

2 Click on the segment you want to delete. It will appear highlighted (darker in EasyDraw). To delete more than one line or patch, hold down the SHIFT key while clicking on lines or patches you want to delete.

3 On the EDIT menu, click Clear. The segment will be gone.

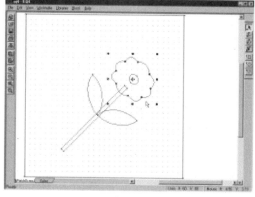

Step 2

 Notes & Tips ─────────────

- You can press the keyboard DELETE key to achieve the same result as Clear.
- **To delete quilts, blocks or fabrics see:** DELETING QUILTS, BLOCKS OR FABRICS FROM THE SKETCHBOOK.
- **To delete entire projects, see:** DELETING PROJECTS.

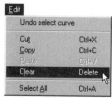

Step 3

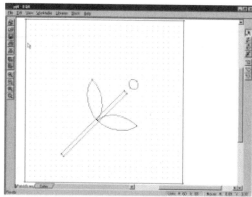

The patch has been deleted.

Part 6
Printing

Part 6
Printing

Printing a Quilt

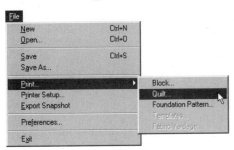

Step 2

Step 3

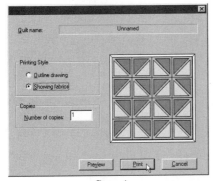

Step 4

Step 3

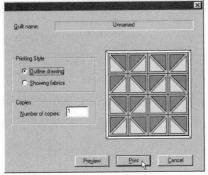

Step 4

You can print your quilt with or without color showing.

Printing a Colored Quilt

1 Have the quilt you have colored on your screen.

2 On the FILE menu, point to Print, click Quilt.

   The Print Quilt box will appear.

3 Under Printing Style, click to select (put a dot in front of) Showing fabrics.

4 Click the Print button.

   If your printer can print in color, it will print a colored picture of your quilt. If your printer prints only in black and white, it will print a black and white shaded quilt.

Printing a Quilt as a Line Drawing

1 Have the quilt on your screen.

2 On the FILE menu, point to Print, click Quilt.

   The Print Quilt box will appear.

3 Under Printing Style, click to select (put a dot in front of) Outline drawing.

4 Click the Print button. Your printer will print a black and white drawing showing an unshaded quilt outline.

💡 **Notes & Tips** ─────────

- **Quilt outlines can be used for quilting classes where students hand-color blocks to determine block and color placement. They also make good coloring book pages for kids.**

- **You can export your quilt picture. See:** EXPORTING SNAPSHOT.

- **You can print a picture of your quilt on the whole computer screen. See:** PRINTING A PICTURE OF THE WHOLE SCREEN.

Printing a Quilt

Printing a Quilting Stencil

Quilting Stencils are blocks that print with a dotted line. The Block Library contains a special section called Quilting Stencils. You can print any of them, to make a quilting design. But you can also turn *any* block into a quilting stencil pattern when you print.

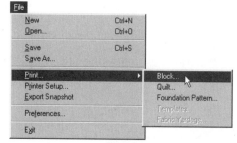

Step 2

1   Be working on a block.

    OR

    If you are working on a quilt, have the block in a quilt, then click the Select tool; click the block on the quilt.

    This selects the block.

2   On the FILE menu, point to Print, click Block.

The Print Block box appears.

3   Click in the Width and Height boxes and type in the finished block size you want. If the "Size from Quilt" box is checked, it means you're printing a block from the quilt and do not need to type in the size.

Note:

**Printing a block right from the quilt?
The Size from Quilt box will automatically be checked. You do not need to type in a size; EQ4 remembers the block size you have set in the quilt layout. To print a different size, uncheck the Size from Quilt box and type the finished block size you want.**

Printing a block from the block worktable? The Size from Quilt box will *not* be checked. You must type in the finished block size you want.

4   Under Printing Style, click to select (put a dot in front of) Quilting stencil.

5   Click Preview to preview your printout.

6   Click Print to print it.

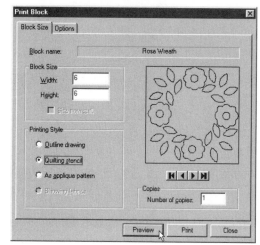

Steps 3-5

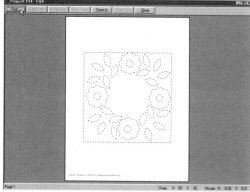

Step 6

Printing a Quilting Stencil

Printing a Block Outline

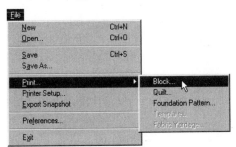

Step 2

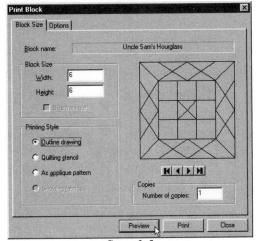

Steps 3-5

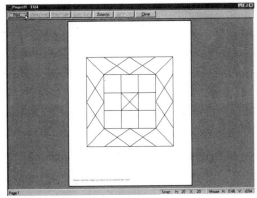

Step 6

You can print a line drawing of any block. These block outlines are handy for classes. Quilting students (or even elementary kids) can hand-color the block, discovering how color placement affects block design.

1   Be working on a block.
    OR
    If you are working on a quilt, have the block in a quilt, then click the Select tool; click the block on the quilt. This selects the block.

2   On the FILE menu, point to Print, click Block. The Print Block box appears.

3   Click in the Width and Height boxes and type in the finished block size you want. If the "Size from Quilt" box is checked, it means you're printing a block from the quilt and do not need to type in the size.

Note:
Printing a block right from the quilt?
The Size from Quilt box will automatically be checked. You do not need to type in a size; EQ4 remembers the block size you have set in the quilt layout. To print a different size, uncheck the Size from Quilt box and type the finished block size you want.
Printing a block from the block worktable?
The Size from Quilt box will *not* be checked. You must type in the finished block size you want.

4   Under Printing Style, click to select (put a dot in front of) Outline drawing.

5   Click Preview to preview your printout.

6   Click Print to print it.

💡 **Notes & Tips** ─────────

- You can print a quilt outline. See: PRINTING A QUILT.
- To print the name of the block on the printout, click the Options tab and click to check the box in front of Print block name.
- To print many small block outlines on the same page, have a small (2 x 2; 3 x 3) size set in the Width and Height boxes, click the Options tab and click to check the box in front of Print as many as fit.

87

Printing a Colored Block

You can print a colored picture of any block.

1   Be working on a block.

    OR

    If you are working on a quilt, have the block in a quilt, then click the Select tool; click the block on the quilt.

    This selects the block.

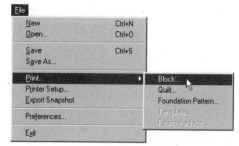

Step 2

2   On the FILE menu, point to Print, click Block.

    The Print Block box appears.

3   Click in the Width and Height boxes and type in the finished block size you want. If the "Size from Quilt" box is checked, it means you're printing a block from the quilt and do not need to type in the size.

Note:
Printing a block right from the quilt?
The Size from Quilt box will automatically be checked. You do not need to type in a size; EQ4 remembers the block size you have set in the quilt layout. To print a different size, uncheck the Size from Quilt box and type the finished block size you want.
Printing a block from the block worktable?
The Size from Quilt box will *not* be checked. You must type in the finished block size you want.

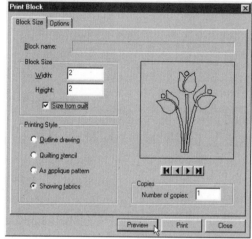

Steps 3-5

4   Under Printing Style, click to select (put a dot in front of) Showing fabrics.

5   Click Preview to preview your printout.

Step 6

6   Click Print to print it.

    If your printer can print in color, it will print a colored picture of your block. If your printer prints only in black and white, it will print a black and white shaded block.

Printing an Applique Pattern

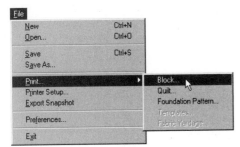

Step 2

Steps 3-5

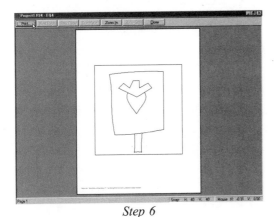

Step 6

An appliqué pattern is an outline drawing of the appliqué block. There is no added seam allowance.

1   Be working on an appliqué block.

   OR

   If you are working on a quilt, have the appliqué block in a quilt, then click the Select tool; click the block on the quilt.

   This selects the block.

2   On the FILE menu, point to Print, click Block.

   The Print Block box appears.

3   Click in the Width and Height boxes and type in the finished block size you want. If the "Size from Quilt" box is checked, it means you're printing a block from the quilt and do not need to type in the size.

Note:
   Printing an appliqué block right from the quilt? The Size from Quilt box will automatically be checked. You do not need to type in a size; EQ4 remembers the block size you have set in the quilt layout. To print a different size, uncheck the Size from Quilt box and type the finished block size you want.

Printing an appliqué block from the block worktable?
The Size from Quilt box will *not* be checked. You must type in the finished block size you want.

4   Under Printing Style, click to select (put a dot in front of) As appliqué pattern.

5   Click Preview to preview your printout.

6   Click Print to print it.

Printing a Foundation Pattern

Foundation Patterns are another name for paper piecing patterns. You'll find a whole category of paper piecing patterns in the EQ4 Block Library, ready for printing. There are many books and Web pages describing the foundation piecing technique of sewing fabric onto these patterns to make blocks.

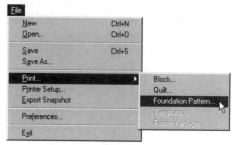

Step 2

1   Be working on a pieced block suitable for foundation piecing (see the Block Library styles in the "3 Paper-Piecing" category.)
OR
If you are working on a quilt, have the block in a quilt, then click the Select tool; click the block on the quilt. This selects the block.

2   On the FILE menu, point to Print, click Foundation Pattern. The Print Foundation box will appear.

Note:
If your block appears on the Numbering tab, but no numbers are showing. It means your block probably can't be effectively foundation pieced. You'll see a message suggesting other printing options. Click Close. Print the block as template patterns. See: PRINTING TEMPLATES.

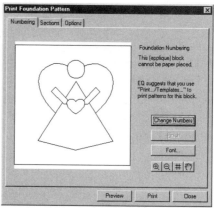

This appliqué block can't be foundation pieced. EQ4 will suggest you print templates.

Numbering

3   Click the Numbering tab. You will see numbers and letters in the sections. The numbers represent the sewing sequence and the letters represent sections.

4   To number the block yourself, on the Numbers tab, click Change Numbers. The numbers and letters will disappear.

5   Click on any section and a number and letter will appear in the section.

Sections

6   Blue-dashed lines surround the areas that have been denoted as sections. Some blocks cannot be automatically numbered because they have more than one section.

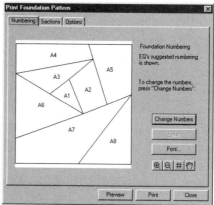

This block is 1 unit so it would open to the Numbering tab.

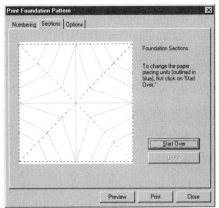

Step 6

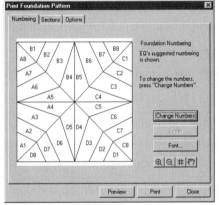

Step 7

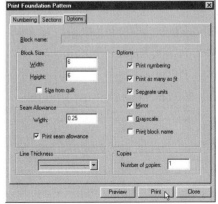

Steps 8-14

These blocks will open to the sections tab.

7   To section the block yourself, on the Sections tab, click Start Over. All blue dashes will disappear. Follow the instructions on screen to section the block yourself. Then go to the Numbering tab to view EQ4's suggested numbers. Change them if you'd like.

8   Click the Options tab. This is where you determine how your block will appear on the printed page.

9   Click in the Width and Height boxes and type in the finished block size you want. If the Size from Quilt box is checked, it means you're printing a block from the quilt and do not need to type in the size.

Note:
    Printing a block right from the quilt? The Size from Quilt box will automatically be checked. You do not need to type in a size; EQ4 remembers the block size you have set in the quilt layout. To print a different size, uncheck the Size from Quilt box and type the finished block size you want.
    Printing a block from the block worktable? The SIze from Quilt box will not be checked. You must type in the finished block size you want.

10   The standard seam allowance is ¼ inch. Follow the procedure in step 9 to change it.

11   To have the seam allowance appear in your printing, click the box beside Print seam allowance so there is a checkmark in it.

12   You can select the Line Thickness for your block printout. Click on the down arrow to view the different line widths. Click one.

13   Under the options box you have several printing choices. To select an option, click the box next to it so a checkmark appears.

14   Click the Print button at any point when you are on the Print Foundation Pattern menu.

Printing a Foundation Pattern

Printing Templates

Templates are block patterns. Each patch is printed as a separate piece, surrounded by seam allowance. You can print templates for any block you have showing on the BLOCK worktable or QUILT worktable.

1   Be working on a block.
    OR
    If you are working on a quilt, have the block in a quilt, then click the Select tool; click the block on the quilt. This selects the block.

2   On the FILE menu, point to Print, click Templates. The Print Templates box appears.

3   Click in the Width and Height boxes and type in the finished block size you want. If the "Size from Quilt" box is checked, it means you're printing a block from the quilt and do not need to type in the size.

Note:

Printing a block right from the quilt? The Size from Quilt box will automatically be checked. You do not need to type in a size; EQ4 remembers the block size you have set in the quilt layout. To print a different size, uncheck the Size from Quilt box and type the finished block size you want.

Printing a block from the block worktable? The Size from Quilt box will *not* be checked. You must type in the finished block size you want.

4   The standard seam allowance is automatically set for you, but you can change it by clicking in the Seam Allowance Width box and typing the size you want. If you do *not* want seam allowance, click to remove the check from the Print seam allowance box.

5   You can select the Line Thickness for your block printout. Click on the down arrow to view the different line widths. Click one.

6   Click Preview to preview your printout.

7   Click Print to print it.

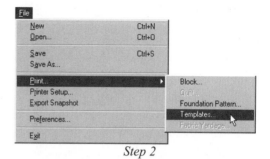

Step 2

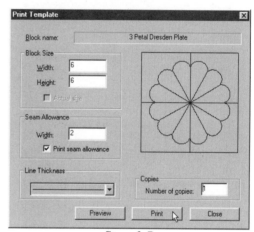

Steps 3-7

Printing a Picture of the Whole Screen

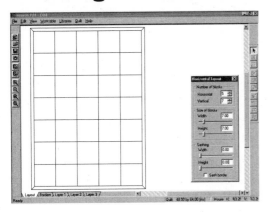

Printing a picture of the whole screen is a good way to remember the settings for a specific quilt layout.

Sometimes you may want to print an entire computer screen to capture rulers, tools, or color palettes plus your block or quilt.

1   With the picture of the screen you want to print on your computer, press the PRINT SCREEN key on your keyboard. You will not see anything happen, but a copy of the picture has been sent to your clipboard.

2   From the Program listings on your computer's hard drive, open a drawing, imaging, or word-processing program. Since there are many different programs we will not cover every one. Instead, we suggest using Paint, WordPad, or Microsoft Word™.

3   Holding down the CTRL key on your keyboard, press the letter V key. Your entire screen capture (from EQ4) will appear in the document.

4   From the FILE menu, click Print. Your EQ4 screen capture will print.

 Notes & Tips ────────────

- Printing the screen is helpful to remember layout settings. Have the layout or border tabs showing when your picture is being copied.
- You can copy the screen when you are in the block or fabric libraries to help you remember where you got a certain block or fabric patch.
- You can change the size of the copied screen by click, holding, and dragging the nodes around the picture from the word processing program.

Part 7
Special Features

Part 7
Special Features

Keeping Design Notes

Step 1

Step 2

Step 4

Finished!

You can save notes along with your block or quilt designs. You must first have blocks or quilts saved in the Sketchbook. See: SAVING BLOCKS OR QUILTS IN THE SKETCHBOOK.

1 Click the View Sketchbook button.

2 Click the Blocks or Quilts tab. In this example, we're using blocks.

3 Click your block, to select it. For quilts, click the arrows until you see your quilt.

4 Click the Notecard button.

5 Press the TAB key on your keyboard. There will be a blinking cursor on the Notecard letting you know where your words will begin when you start typing.

6 Type a name for your block or quilt in the name field.

7 Press the TAB key again to move to Reference; press TAB again to move to Notes.

Note:
If you accidentally tab more than twice and "lose" your cursor, don't worry. Just press the TAB key repeatedly until your cursor appears where you want it.

8 Type as many notes you would like here.

9 Click the Close (X) button in the upper-right corner. You're back to your Sketchbook.

10 Click the Close (X) button to close the Sketchbook.

Saving Notecards

To permanently save your block or quilt notes, save your project (see: SAVING A PROJECT), or save your block in the block library (see: SAVING BLOCKS IN THE LIBRARY).

Printing Notecards

To print out notes, select, copy (CTRL+C) and paste (CTRL+V) the Name, Reference, or Notes information of the notecard in a word processor document.

Keeping Design Notes

Exporting Snapshot

Making a snapshot is like taking a picture of part of the screen. You can open your snapshot picture in another program, print it, or even change it into a bitmap file to use in other software (perhaps to machine embroidery!)

Step 1

1   Click the Export Snapshot button. Nothing will happen, but the cursor will look like a magnifying glass with a crosshair in the center.

2   Click, hold, and drag the cursor from the top-left of the image you want to capture to the bottom-right. As you drag the cursor you will see a dotted rectangle form showing you what you are capturing.

3   Release the mouse. You will see an Export Snapshot pop-up menu appear with three choices explained below.

Step 2

Save as bitmap file

1   Click the Save as bitmap file button. A standard Windows file directory will appear.

2   Find the folder you'd like to save the bitmap image in by double-clicking on the respective folder icons.

3   Name the bitmap. The File name field will be highlighted. Begin typing to replace the existing name with the new name.

4   Click Save. Your image will be saved.

Copy to Windows clipboard

1   Click the Copy to Windows clipboard. You will not see anything happen, but your image has been copied to the clipboard.

2   From the Program listings on your computer's harddrive, open a drawing, imaging, or word-processing program.

3   On a new page, hold down the CTRL key, and press the letter "V" (Paste). Your captured image will appear in the docu-

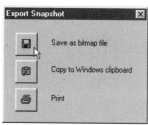

Step 1

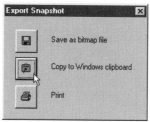

Step 2

ment.

Print

1 Click the Print button. Your captured image will print.

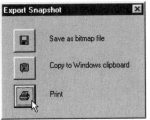

Step 1

 Notes & Tips ————————————

- Saving your exported snapshot as a bitmap file you can use it in a graphics or imaging software program. Specifically, you could use it in a sewing software program to make embroidery patterns.
- Copying an exported snapshot to a Windows document you can add text and make a note for a friend or create a newsletter.
- You can combine more than one snapshot on a page, especially after resizing.
- Copying an exported snapshot to a Windows document you can attach it and send it to other people using e-mail.
- You can make labels if you copy a snapshot to a Windows document. See: MAKING LABELS.
- Printing a snapshot is helpful to view magnified images.
- If you print snapshots you will see everthing the camera captured on the screen, including guidelines and grid points. This is helpful in determining sizing and spacing of images.
- You can print the entire screen. See: PRINTING A PICTURE OF THE WHOLE SCREEN.
- If you want to magnify a section of a design, but you don't want to export it you can zoom in. See: ZOOMING IN AND ZOOMING OUT.

Exporting Snapshot

Importing Scanned Fabrics

To use scanned fabric in EQ4 you must have access to a scanner, scan the fabric, and save it on your computer. You must also have an imaging software program. Since there are many different kinds of scanners we will not tell you how to scan the fabric (you will need to read your scanner's manual for that). However, we will give you suggestions on how to save the scanned fabric and what you can do with the fabric once you have it scanned.

There are numerous variables to determine when scanning. Many of these variables will be decided by what kind of scanner and image-editing program you have.

Yet, the following points are worthy of a note:

A Iron the fabric so there are no wrinkles. Wrinkles will show up in scanned fabrics.

B Save the fabric as a bitmap image (bmp).

C Save the fabric using a 256-color bitmap.

D Save the fabric with a pixel size no larger than 200x200.

E You may have to resize the scanned fabric. For example, if you scan a fabric with a big print you may have to scan it at 50%, instead of 100%, to see more of the print.

Once the Fabric is Scanned

1 On the LIBRARIES menu, on a quilt or block layout, click Fabric Library. The Fabric Libraries pop-up menu will appear.

2 On the Fabric Libraries pop-up menu, click Import. A pop-up directory menu will appear.

3 On the pop-up directory menu, click on the respective folders where you saved your scanned fabric, click the fabric, and click Open. The fabric swatch will appear in the Fabric Libraries' Style box.

4 Click Copy. The fabric swatch will disappear from the Style box and will now

Step 1

The Fabric Libraries box as it first appears.

Step 2

Step 3

Step 4

be in the Sketchbook and the Color and Fabric palette. The new scanned fabric will be the last swatch in both the sketchbook and on the palette.

Step 5

5   On the Fabric Libraries pop-up menu, click Close. You will be back at your quilt or block layout.

At this point you can:

•   Color patches, blocks or quilts with the new fabric. See: COLORING A BLOCK or COLORING A QUILT.

•   Save your fabric in the library. See: SAVING FABRICS IN THE LIBRARY.

•   Make different colorways using the new fabric. See: MAKING PRINT FABRICS IN NEW COLORWAYS.

Importing Scanned Fabrics

Importing Bitmaps

If you have a picture you would like to use for a block you can bring it into EQ4 (import it) and trace over it, looking at the picture as you draw. The picture must be saved on your computer as a bitmap graphic. You can trace a bitmap with the EasyDraw (for pieced blocks) or PatchDraw (for applique blocks) tools.

1 On the WORKTABLE menu, click Work on Block.

2 On the BLOCK menu, point to New Block, click EasyDraw or PatchDraw.

Note:
If you import a design to draw as a pieced block, you would select the Easy Draw tools. Use PatchDraw for applique.

3 On the BLOCK menu, click Import for Tracing. A pop-up directory menu will appear.

Note:
To import your bitmap, you must know where you saved it on your computer.

4 Click the down arrow beside the "Look in" box, and scroll to find your bitmap.

5 Click the folder where you saved your bitmap. Click Open.

6 Click on your .bmp and click on Open. You will be back to your block, the image will be imported, and you will be on a new tab called Bitmap.

Cropping and Resizing

Before beginning to trace the image you will probably need to crop and resize the graphic. To crop a graphic is to select part of an image and discard the rest. Specifically, you are trying to get rid of any excess image around the edges that you do not want to be part of your block.

Step 1

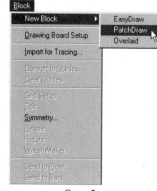

Step 2

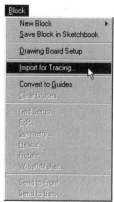

Step 3

Step 4   *Step 5*

Step 6

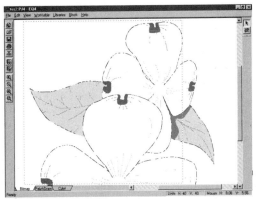

Dogwood.bmp looks like this when you first import it.

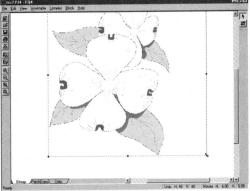

Step 8

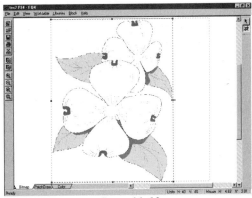

Steps 11-12

Resizing

7 Click the Resize tool and click on the graphic.

8 Click, hold, and drag the node at the bottom-right corner. (The cursor will change to a double-sided arrow.) Drag until the graphic fills the entire block space. (The edges of the graphic should match the edge lines of the block.) Release the mouse button.

9 Click the PatchDraw (or EasyDraw) tab. The graphic will appear in the block. At this point you are ready to crop or trace your imported graphic.

Cropping

10 Click on the Crop tool and then click on the graphic. (A dotted line will surround the image.)

11 Click, hold, and drag a node on the dotted line. (The cursor changes into a double-sided arrow.) Make sure its edges are even with the edges of the graphic.

Note:
It is helpful to drag the image into the middle of the block (by clicking on, holding, and dragging the picture away from the corner) so you can see the edges of the graphic more clearly.

12 Once the edges surrounding the border are even with those of the image, return the graphic to the upper-left corner of the block. (Again, select the graphic and drag it to the corner.)

Importing Bitmaps

103

Tracing Bitmaps

We'll trace a flower to illustrate typical tracing steps. In Patchdraw you can overlap patches, so before you begin tracing an applique image, take a minute to look at how the patches will be layered in the drawing. Although you can change the layering of patches when you color (see: LAYERING PATCHES), it is easier to keep them in order when you initially trace them. First-drawn = bottom; last-drawn = top.

1   On the Simple ovals tool button, click the little black triangle in the top-left corner, and click on a leaf shape.

2   Click, hold, and drag to make a general outline of one of the dogwood leaves. Since the outline is probably not exact, you can edit the shape to make a better leaf.

3   Click the Bezier edit tool.

4   Click the leaf outline you just drew. You'll note only one side of the leaf is highlighted and it has two handle nodes.

5   Click, hold, and drag one of the handle nodes to see how it reshapes the leaf. Move both handle nodes until it closely traces the bitmap image.

6   Click the other side of the leaf so it is highlighted.

7   Move the handle nodes so that the edges of the leaf drawing match the image.

8   Repeat steps 1-7 for the other leaves.

9   On the Simple ovals tool button, click the little black triangle in the top-left corner, and click on the heart shape.

10 Click, hold, and drag from the outside of a petal toward the inside of the flower.

11 Click the Bezier edit tool.

12 Click the heart. Again, only one side is highlighted with two handle nodes at either end.

Step 1

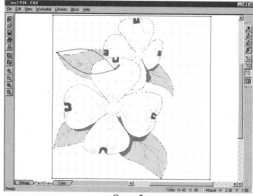

Step 2

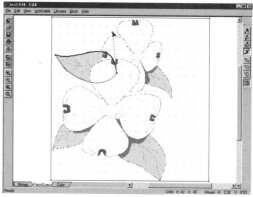

Steps 4-7

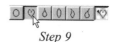

Step 9

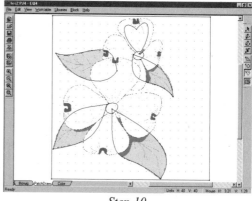

Step 10

Tracing Bitmaps

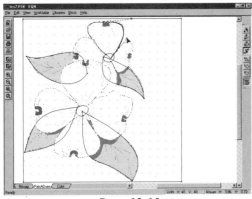

Steps 12-15

Step 17

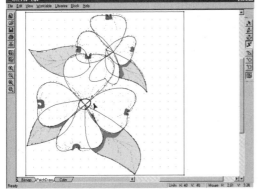

Steps 20-22

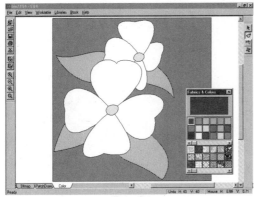

Step 24

13 Click, hold, and drag one of the handle nodes or one of the nodes directly on the shape outline to see how it reshapes the heart. Move nodes until it closely traces the bitmap image.

14 Click the other side of the heart so it is highlighted.

15 Move the nodes so that the edges of the heart drawing match the petals of the image.

16 Repeat steps 9-15 for the other petals.

17 On the Simple ovals tool, click the little triangle in the top left corner, and click the circle.

18 Click, hold, and drag over the center of one of the flowers.

19 Click the Bezier edit tool.

20 Click the circle so that one side is high-lighted with nodes.

21 Click, hold, and drag any of the nodes to reshape the circle to match the center of the flower.

22 Click and reshape the other side of the circle.

23 Repeat steps 17-22 for the other center.

24 Click on the Color tab and color your beautiful design.

Notes & Tips

• **You can click on the Show/Hide Bitmap button (the cactus) to make the bitmap image appear and disappear. Hiding the bitmap image lets you see only the lines you have drawn.**

Tracing Bitmaps

Fussy Cutting Fabric

Fussy Cutting is a quilter's term for being "fussy" about cutting out fabric print motifs (leaves, flowers, cats etc). For example, if you cut out fabric with cats "just so," to center a cat in a patch, you are "fussy cutting."

You can "fussy cut" fabric designs in EQ4, sliding fabric around to center motifs precisely, making your blocks look perfect on screen. To use the Fussy Cut tool you must have a colored block (not quilt) showing on screen, then start at step 6. If you do not yet have a block showing, follow steps 1 - 5 below, to get a block.

Step 1

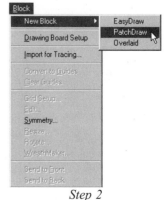

Step 2

1   On the WORKTABLE menu, click Work on Block.

2   On the BLOCK menu, point to New Block, click EasyDraw, PatchDraw or Overlaid.

Step 4

3   Get a block from the Block Library showing on the block worktable. See: GETTING A BLOCK FROM THE LIBRARY; then see: GETTING BLOCKS/QUILTS FROM THE SKETCHBOOK. OR
Draw your own block.

Step 6

4   Click the Color tab.

5   Color your block. See: COLORING A BLOCK. Use print fabrics, to see the fabrics move.

6   Click the Fussy Cut tool.

7   Click any fabric print patch in your block, then hold down the left mouse button and drag the mouse on the patch. The fabric "drags" on the patch as you move the mouse. Release the mouse when you're done fussy cutting.

💡 **Notes & Tips**

• **Fussy Cutting works only on blocks. (Your perfectly arranged fabric will shift when you set the blocks into quilts, because the block size changes dramatically.)**

• **Use Fussy Cutting to make your blocks "picture perfect" before you take a "snapshot" of them for exporting. See:** EXPORTING SNAPSHOT.

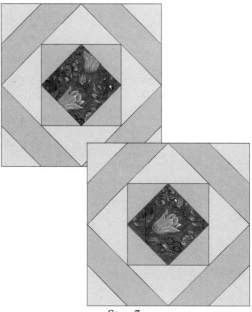

Step 7

Notice how the fabric has been moved with the Fussy Cut tool.

Part 8
Miscellaneous

Part 8
Miscellaneous

Zooming In and Zooming Out

Step 1

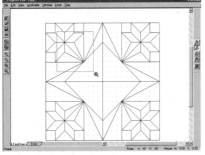

Step 2

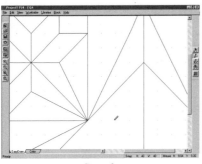

Step 3

The Zoom Out tool

The Fit to Window tool

The Refresh Screen tool

Zooming In

Zooming in means to magnify a section of your block or quilt.

1   Click the Zoom In tool.

2   Click and hold your mouse at the top-left of the area you would like to magnify and diagonally drag the mouse to the bottom-right corner of the area. (You will see a rectangle forming around the area.)

3   Release the mouse. The screen will be redrawn to magnify the selected area.

4   You may zoom closer in by repeating steps 2–3.

Zooming Out

To zoom out is to return your view to the previous magnification.

1   Click the Zoom Out tool. The drawing will return to its previous magnification. If you zoom in 3 times, you zoom out 3 times to return to return to normal.

Fit to Window

To return to normal view in 1 click, use the Fit to Window tool.

Refresh Screen

Clicking the Refresh Screen button redraws the screen. You'll find this button helpful if your drawing board needs "cleaning."

Choosing Inches or Centimeters

You can use inch or centimeter measurements in EQ4.

1 On the FILE menu, click Preferences. The Preferences dialog box will appear, with tabs.

2 Click the Measurement tab.

3 Click in the circle to the left of either Inches or Centimeters. A black dot will appear in the circle. The other circle will be blank or white.

 Notes & Tips ————————————

- **Once you change the measurement units the program will continue to use those units until you change them.**

Step 1

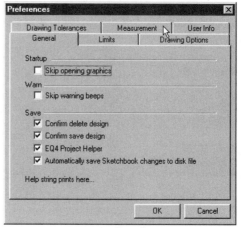

Step 2

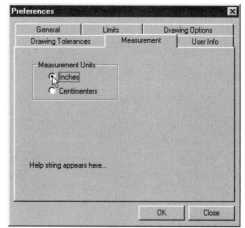

Step 3

Sorting Colors or Fabrics

Step 1

Step 2

Step 3
"Right click" to get this pop-up menu.

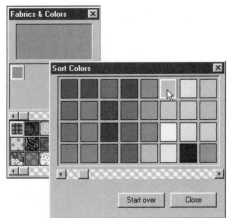

Step 4
Choose colors in the order that you want them.

Sorting the colors or fabrics arranges them in the order *you* want, letting you put your favorites up front in the Fabrics & Colors palette. To sort either colors or fabrics you must have the Fabrics & Colors palette open.

1 On the WORKTABLE menu, click Work on Quilt.

2 Click the Paintbrush tool.

3 On the Fabrics and Colors palette, click with the *right* mouse button. A pop-up menu appears.

4 Click Sort Colors. A Sort Colors box appears with the color swatches in it.

5 Click the color swatches in the order you want them sorted. The first swatch clicked will appear first in your palette. When you click on a swatch, it will "disappear" so you won't select the same color twice.

6 Continue clicking color swatches until you have sorted all you wish.

Note: If you make a mistake, click the Start Over button. This puts the swatches you've already sorted back into the very end of the sorting box. You can begin sorting again.

7 Click the Close button.

8 Click the Paintbrush tool. You will see the colors in the order you clicked on them.

Sorting fabrics is exactly the same as sorting colors except you right-click on a fabric swatch and choose Sort Fabrics. The remaining steps are all the same.

Notes & Tips

- **The sorted color order gets saved when you save your project.**
- **When you start a new project, the colors will be in their normal (default) order.**

111

Creating New Colors

If you can't find just the right solid colors you
need for your block, you can create your own
colors.

1 On the WORKTABLE menu, click Work
on Quilt.

2 Click the Paintbrush tool.

3 Place the cursor over a color swatch (don't
click). You will see a RGB number appear.
The number, different for every swatch,
represents the amount of red (R), green
(G), and blue (B) in each color. The palette
can range from black (R:0, G:0, B:0) to
white (R:255, G:255, B:255). Every
combination does not exist in the Sketch-
book/palette, but it can be made.

4 *Right*-click on any color swatch and click
on Add Colors. A Color menu appears
with 48 basic colors.

5 On the Color menu, click on Define
Custom Colors. A square with a rainbow
will appear (as well as some other number
fields). The rainbow looks blurry because
the colors are running together displaying
every RGB combination that the program
can make. To the right of the rainbow is a
vertical scroll bar. If you click on one of
the 48 basic colors you will see the
variations of that color on the scroll bar
along with its respective RGB number
underneath.

6 Click on any color swatch closest in color
to the new color you want to make.

7 Click on, hold, and drag the slider-bar
arrow up. You will see the RGB numbers
change, as well as the Color/Solid box that
displays the corresponding color.

8 When you see a color you like in the
Color/Solid box, click on the Add to
Custom Colors button. Your new color will
pop up in the Custom Colors box.

Step 1

Step 2

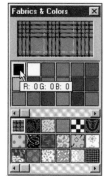

Step 5
*See how the values for Red,
Green and Blue are all set
to 0 to make black.*

Step 6
*"Right Click" any color
swatch to get this menu.*

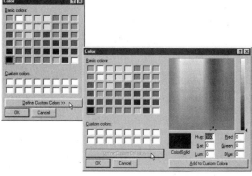

Clicking on Define Custom Colors *will expand
the "Basic Colors" box to show the color
rainbow and RGB values.*

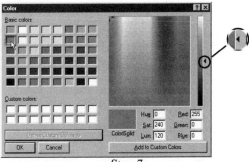

Step 7

Drag the slider bar up and down to see the color change.

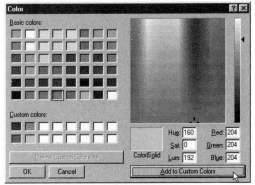

Steps 10-11

The Custom Colors you just added are now under the Basic colors. You can add up to 16 Custom Colors each time you use this box.

Note:

You can manually type in any RGB number. Place your cursor in front of the number in the Red box and click the mouse button (the cursor will be flashing). Hold down the mouse button, click and drag the cursor over the number (the number will appear highlighted). Type the number you want (as soon as you start typing the original/highlighted number will disappear). Press the TAB key and it will take you down to the Green box automatically highlighting the number for you so that all you have to do is type in the number.

Press the TAB key again to enter the number in the Blue box and then click OK to see your new color appear.

11 Repeat steps 7 and 8 to add up to 16 new colors.

12 Click on OK. You will be back looking at the Colors and Fabrics palette.

💡 **Notes & Tips** ────────────

- Another way to instantly make additional colors is by getting fabrics from the Fabric Library. You will automatically get new solid colors coordinating with the fabrics you choose.

Creating a Shaded Palette

You can create a shaded color palette, light to dark, to color with. For example, perhaps you want ten blues, ranging from light blue to dark blue. Here's how you pick out a color and create light to dark shades of that color.

Step 1

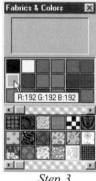

Step 2

1   On the WORKTABLE menu, click Work on Quilt.

2   Click the Paintbrush tool. The Fabrics and Colors palette will appear.

3   Place the cursor over a color swatch (don't click). You will see a RGB number appear. The number, different for every swatch, represents the amount of red (R), green (G), and blue (B) in each color. The palette can range from black which is R:0, G:0, B:0 to white which is R:255, G:255, B:255. Every combination does not exist in the palette, but it can be made.

Step 3

Step 4

4   *Right*-click on any color swatch. Click on Add Colors. A Color menu appears with 48 basic colors.

5   On the Color menu, click on Define Custom Colors. A square with a rainbow will appear. The rainbow looks blurry because the colors are running together displaying every RGB combination the program can make. To the right of the rainbow is a vertical scroll bar. If you click on one of the 48 basic colors you will see the variations of that color on the scroll bar along with its respective RGB number underneath.

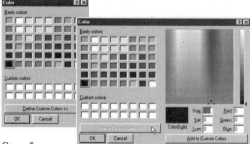

Step 5

Clicking on the Define Custom Colors button expands your color choices dramatically.

6   Click on any color square that you would like to create a shaded palette for.

7   Click on, hold, and drag the slider-bar arrow (which is beside the vertical scroll bar) to the top (the Color/Solid will be white and the RGB will all be at 255).

8   Click ¼ of an inch below the arrow. The arrow will "jump" down and you will see a very light pastel appear in the color/solid

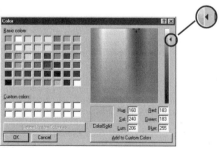

Step 7

You can click and drag this arrow or you can type in the RGB numbers by hand.

Creating a Shaded Palette

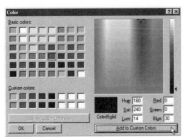

Steps 9 & 10
In our example, we've chosen 10 shades of
blue for our shaded palette.

Step 11
Our 10 new shades are now at the end of the
default colors in the Fabrics & Colors palette.

box.

9   Click Add to Custom Colors. The new color will appear in the first (top-left) box under Custom colors.

10   Repeat steps 7–9 as many times as you want (up to 16) for the original swatch. Remember, each added custom color will show up in your palette.

11   Click OK. Your added shades will be at the end of the palette.

💡 Notes & Tips

- If you don't want your new shades/colors at the end of the palette you can sort your color swatches (see: SORTING COLORS OR FABRICS).
- The Custom colors can hold up to 16 new colors. Therefore, when the 16 boxes are filled up you need to click OK to save your new colors, then repeat the steps to use the Add colors tool.

Creating a Shaded Palette

Making Labels

There are many word processing, graphic, and greeting-card software programs. It is impossible to cover every program, so for this recipe we are going to use Microsoft Word™ because it has an envelopes and labels tool. You may try the steps in this recipe in any software program. To begin this recipe you must copy a picture to the Windows clipboard using the Export Snapshot tool. See: EXPORTING A SNAPSHOT.

1 With your snapshot copied and pasted on a Word™ document, click on the snapshot. Nodes will surround the snapshot.

2 Click, hold, and drag the bottom right node diagonally until your snapshot is about ¾ inch square.

3 On the FORMAT menu, click Picture. On the Position tab, click on Float over text so the checkmark disappears. All of the fields will go gray. Click OK.

4 On the EDIT menu, click Copy. You will not see anything happen, but your snapshot has been copied to the clipboard.

5 On the TOOLS menu, click Envelopes and Labels. The Envelopes and Labels menu will appear.

6 Click on the Labels tab.

7 On the Labels tab, click Options. This is where you select the size of your label.

8 For this recipe, we'll use the Avery standard, 8161 address. In the Label products dialog box, click the down arrow and click on Avery standard. In the Product number dialog box, click the down arrow until you find 8161 - Address. Click OK. You will be back on the Labels tab.

9 On the Labels tab, under Print, click on the circle beside Full page of the same label.

Step 2

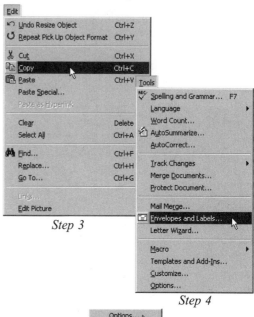

Step 3

Step 4

Step 6

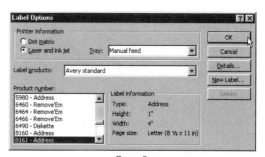

Step 8

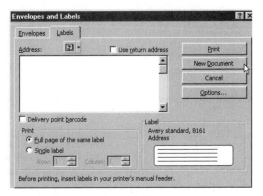

Steps 9-10

Step 13

Step 15

10 On the Labels tab, click New Document. A new document with the label outlines will appear. Your cursor will be blinking in the top-left label outline.

11 On the EDIT menu, click Paste. Your snapshot will appear.

Note:
If your snapshot is too big, click on it. Then, click, hold, and drag on one of the nodes until the snapshot fits in the label outline.

12 Click your keyboard TAB key to the next label outline.

13 On the EDIT menu, click Paste.

14 Repeat steps 11-12 to paste a copy of your snapshot in each label. (You can use different snapshots for each label if you want.)

15 Click the Printer icon. Your snapshots will be printed as labels.

Note:
You will be sending your labels through the printer twice: once with your snapshot, and once with the name and address text. (If you are using other software programs you might be able to combine the snapshot with your text and copy it into the label outline printing it only once.)

16 Open a new page of Avery standard 8161 address labels (note steps 4-9). We will type in the name and address text.

17 Either press your keyboard SPACE BAR or use the tab set (if you know how) to leave space for your snapshot (about an inch).

18 Type the name and address you'd like to appear on the labels.

19 Repeat step 17 for each label.

20 Place your sheet of labels with the printed picture of your snapshot in the printer. Note what side of the sheet of labels needs to go in first and be facing up or down. (It's a good idea to use scrap paper first.)

21 Click the printer icon. You will have beautiful labels!

Making Labels

117

Making Print Fabric in New Colorways

You can change the colors in any fabric–creating new colorways. You'll wish you could do this with real fabric!

Step 1

1 On the WORKTABLE menu, click Work on Quilt.

2 Click the Paintbrush tool. The Fabrics & Colors palette will appear.

3 Click on any print fabric swatch you'd like to make in a new colorway.

4 Point to the same swatch and click on it with the *right* mouse button. A menu appears.

5 Click on Add Colorway. The Add Fabric Colorway box appears. You will see the Original fabric and the New colorway. You haven't changed anything yet, so they look the same.

6 Under the "To this color" box, click on the arrows to change the colors in the print.

7 Click on the Add button to keep a print colorway you like. You may add as many new colorways as you want.

8 Click the Close button to close the box.

9 Click the Paintbrush tool again to make the palette reappear. Click, hold, and drag the slider to the end of the fabrics to see your new colorway.

Step 5

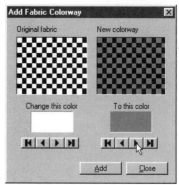

Step 6

The Change this color box shows your the original color. The To this color box shows what the original color will be changed to. Here we've changed the white in this checkered fabric into a dark grey.

💡 **Notes & Tips** ──────────────

- **Your new fabric swatches will be "last in line" in the palette. If you'd prefer them up front, sort the fabrics. See:** SORTING COLORS OR FABRICS.

- **If you want fabrics in colors that aren't available, make the solid colors you need and then repeat these steps. See:** CREATING NEW COLORS. **The last new colorway option (click on the *absolute-right arrow*) will be the original fabric added to the new color you made.**

- **You can save the new fabric colorways in the library so it is available for use later. See:** SAVING FABRICS IN THE LIBRARY.

Step 9

The new colorway is now at the end of the default fabrics.

Part 9

Recipes

Part 9
Recipes

Part 9
Block Recipes

Part 9
Block Recipes

Drawing a Drunkard's Path Block

Step 1

Step 2

Step 3

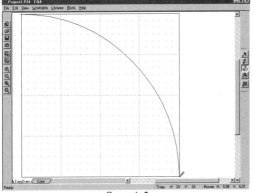

Step 4-5

Drunkard's Path is a pieced block, so it is drawn in EasyDraw, which draws semi-circular curves — easily pieced. (Compare this to the free curves used to draw flowers, for example. For appliqué curves you use PatchDraw.)

To get ready to use EasyDraw for an easy block:

1 Click WORKTABLE, choose Work on Block.

2 Click Block, point to New Block, click EasyDraw. You now have the EasyDraw tools.

To draw a semi-circle for Drunkard's Path, or Fan:

3 Click on the Arc tool.

4 Point the mouse cursor so the pencil point is right in one corner of your drawing square. (Not out from the corner – right *in* the corner.)

5 Holding down the left mouse button, drag the mouse diagonally across the block, until you have an arc that touches the opposite corner of the square. Release the mouse. You will have a Drunkard's Path, or Fan, arc.

 Notes & Tips

• **To change the arc's direction from an "innie" to an "outie," press the keyboard Spacebar** *while drawing the arc.*

• **To draw small Drunkard's Path blocks inside a 4-patch or 9-patch grid, see the section on drawing a grid, draw the grid, then use the Arc tool to draw small curves inside each grid square.**

Drawing an Easy Applique Flower

One way of drawing a flower starts with a shape.

1 On the WORKTABLE menu, click Work on Block.

2 On the BLOCK menu, point to New Block, click PatchDraw.

3 On the Polygon tool, click the small black triangle in the top-left corner. A toolbar showing shape options pops out.

4 Click on any shape.

5 Click, hold, and drag the mouse. You will see your polygon forming. Make the polygon any size you want.

6 On the Bezier edit tool, click the small black square in the bottom-left corner. An Edit Arc menu will pop-up.

Right now each side of your polygon is straight. However, we want to curve the edges so they resemble flower petals.

7 Click any side of your polygon. The side will be highlighted (appear darker).

8 On the Edit Arc menu, click toCurve. Nothing happens to the straight edge/side, but two handle nodes are added.

9 Click, hold, and drag outward on one of the new (handle) nodes. Notice the curve it starts to make.

10 Click, hold, and drag the other node outward to create the full arch or your first petal.

11 Repeat steps 7-10 for each side of your polygon.

12 On the Simple ovals tool, click the small black triangle in the top-left corner. A toolbar showing shape options pops out.

13 Click on the circle.

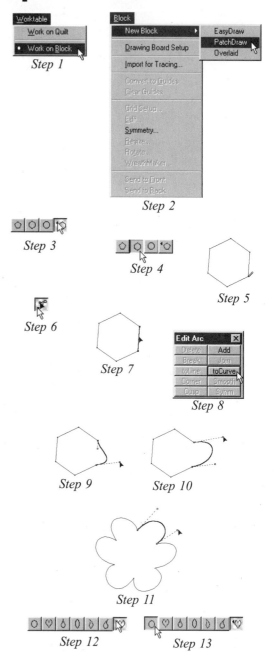

Step 1

Step 2

Step 3

Step 4

Step 5

Step 6

Step 7

Step 8

Step 9

Step 10

Step 11

Step 12

Step 13

Step 14
the completed flower

14 Click, hold, and drag the mouse in the center of your polygon to complete the flower.

 Notes & Tips ───────────

- There are other ways you can make a flower or blossom. However, we think using shapes to create new shapes (i.e., a polygon into a flower) is a neat trick! Plus you know your shape is closed.

- You can create more arcs or flower petals by clicking Add on the Edit Arc pop-up menu when a side is selected (this splits the side into two sections). You will still need to click on toCurve for both sections to form separate arcs.

Drawing an Easy Applique Flower

Drawing a Heart Flower

1 On the WORKTABLE menu, click Work on Block.

2 On the Block menu, point to New Block, click PatchDraw.

3 On the PatchDraw tool bar, click the Simple ovals tool.

Note:
The shape you see on this tool will be any one of six possible patch shapes. EQ4 will "remember" the patch you click on, and will show you that patch next time.

4 On the Simple ovals tool, click the small black triangle in the upper-left corner. A pop-up tool bar will appear with 6 oval shapes. Click on the heart shape.

5 Place your cursor near the top and halfway across the block.

6 Holding down the mouse, drag the cursor straight down to above the center of the block.

7 Release the mouse and you will have a heart. This will be a small flower petal. To make sure the heart petals are the same size, we'll copy the original heart.

8 Click on the Select tool.

9 Click on the heart. Nodes will appear around the heart.

10 On the Select tool, click the small black square in the lower-left corner. The Symmetry menu will appear.

11 Click the Clone button. An exact copy of the first heart will appear. For this heart flower we are going to have 4 petals. Each heart will face toward the center. Therefore, we need to change the direction of the second heart (which should still be selected).

12 Click the Rot 90 button. The heart will rotate 90 degrees. Now you need to move

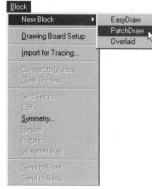

Step 1

Step 2

Step 4

Step 7

Step 11

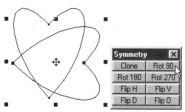

Step 12

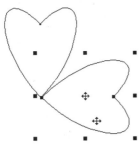

Step 13

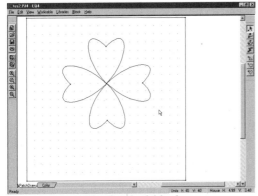

The finished block.

the heart into place.

13 Place your cursor inside the heart and, holding down the mouse button, drag the heart until the point matches with the original heart's point in the center of the block.

14 Repeat steps 11-13 two more times.

Drawing Grandmother's Flower Garden

1 On the WORKTABLE menu, click Work on Block.

2 On the BLOCK menu, point to New Block, click PatchDraw.

3 On the Polygon tool, click on the small black triangle in the upper-left corner. A toolbar showing shape options pops out.

4 Click the hexagon (the center shape).

5 Place your pointer above and to the left of the center of the block (approximately a half inch). Click, hold, and drag the mouse down diagonally. You will see your polygon forming. The shape can be any size, but you'll need to have enough space to fit 6 more same-sized hexagons around the original.

At this point we could draw six more hexagons and connect them to our original hexagon to form our block. However, the sizes may differ. Therefore, we are going to copy our original hexagon to ensure each shape is exactly the same size.

6 Click the Select tool.

7 Click on the hexagon. Nodes will appear around the hexagon.

8 On the EDIT menu, click Copy. Nothing happens.

9 On the EDIT menu, click Paste. You will see a second hexagon appear that looks exactly like the first hexagon.

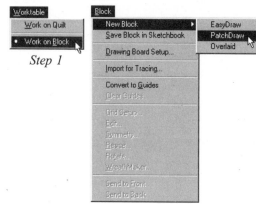

Step 1

Step 1

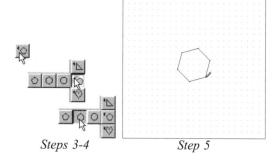

Steps 3-4

Step 5

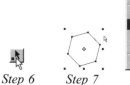

Step 6 *Step 7*

Step 8

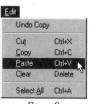

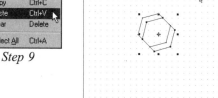

Step 9

128

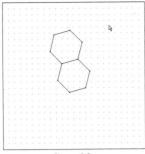

Step 10

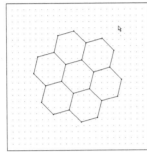

Step 11

10 While the new hexagon is selected, click, hold, and drag it so that one of the edges of the new hexagon matches up with an edge of the original hexagon.

11 You will repeat steps 9-10 five times (except, you will change which side of the original hexagon you paste the new hexagon to) until each edge of the original hexagon has a pasted hexagon attached.

Note
 If the original hexagon does not paste, include steps 6-8 too. You will now have Grandmother's Flower Garden – Congratulations!

At this point you can:

- Color the block. See: COLORING A BLOCK.

- Add a stem with leaves to the flower. See: DRAWING A VINE WITH LEAVES.

- You can create the grandmother's flower garden pattern in a quilt. See: COLORING A FLOWER GARDEN GRID.

💡 **Notes & Tips**

- You can draw guidelines to help you center your pattern. See: MAKING DRAWING GUIDES or DRAWING A GRID.
- If the lines seem to disappear while you are pasting, click the Refresh tool to see what has changed.

Drawing Grandmother's Flower Garden

Making a Wreath

Making original wreath designs for applique and quilting is easy using the WreathMaker. First you make a "drag and drop" patch. Next you let the WreathMaker repeat and rotate this patch. It makes an instant wreath!

1   On the WORKTABLE menu, click Work on Block.

2   On the BLOCK menu, point to New Block, click PatchDraw.

3   On the Simple ovals tool, click on the little black triangle in the top-left corner and click on one of the shapes.

4   Holding down the mouse, drag the mouse to create a small shape anywhere on the block.

5   Click the Select tool.

Tip:
Pressing the keyboard SPACEBAR will select the patch and change the tool for you automatically.

6   Click the shape you just drew. This selects it.

7   *Right*-click anywhere on the selected patch (a flyout menu appears) and click on WreathMaker.

8   Under Number in wreath, click, hold, and drag the slider bar to any position.

9   Under Cluster spacing, click, hold, and drag the slider bar to any position.

10 Under Resize cluster, click, hold, and drag the slider bar to any position.

Step 1

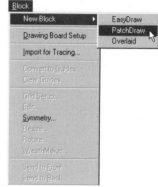

Step 2

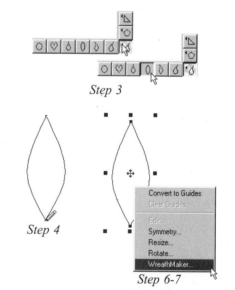

Step 3

Step 4

Step 6-7

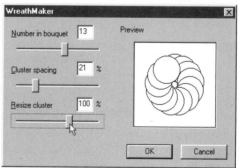

Steps 8-10

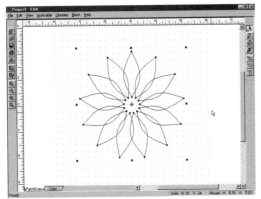

Step 11

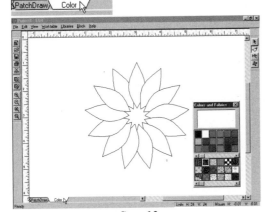

Step 12

Steps 14-15

11 Click OK and watch the wreath appear in the middle of the block! Your wreath will probably not look like our picture.

Note:
When you're looking at the wreath in the Applique/PatchDraw screen it may appear busy near the center because all the nodes are gathered there. Click on the Color tab and you'll see a clearer view of the wreath.

12 Click the Color tab to see your wreath without nodes. If one patch appears on top of another (the spiral stair effect), you can change the layering within the block if you want.

13 Click the Select tool.

14 Click the patch you want to reposition/re-layer.

15 On the BLOCK menu, click Send to Front (or Send to Back). The leaf will now look like it is on top of the other patches (or behind).

Note:
The WreathMaker has 3 fields:

Number in Wreath = **Number of patches (or patch groups) in the wreath. Range: 3 - 20**

Cluster Spacing = **Amount of space between patches. Range: 0 - 100%**

Wreaths are automatically centered in the block. A value of 0% represents no spacing. Specifically, this means the lower center point of the select box rotates around the center point of the block. A value of 100% pushes the clusters as far to the outside edge of the block as possible (which may require the cluster to be made smaller).

Resize Cluster = **Amount the cluster is resized. The maximum value for resize depends on the size of the original select. If the original select is small, the maximum resize is 300%. If the original select is large, the maximum value will vary.**

Now you may want to see:

SAVING A BLOCK IN THE BLOCK LIBRARY

WREATH RECIPES

Making a Wreath

131

Wreath Recipes

Start out with this simple oval to make the following wreath designs.

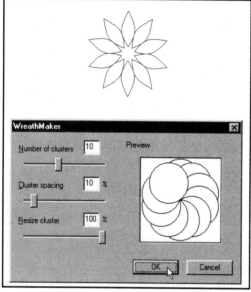

See what happens when you change the angle of the Simple Oval to a 45° angle (fig. A), or a 90° angle (fig. B).

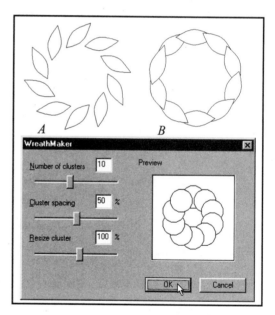

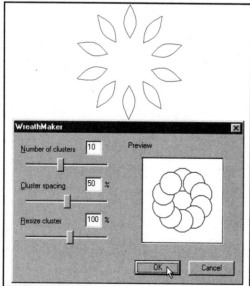

Wreath Recipes

Start out with this simple oval to make the following wreath designs.

Sometimes, drawing a shape differently, or rotating, can have a big effect on the finished wreath.

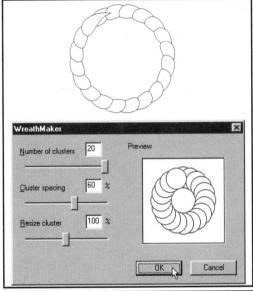

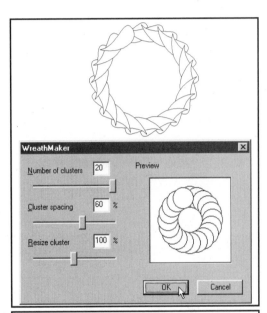

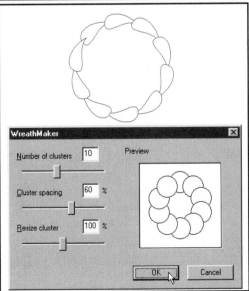

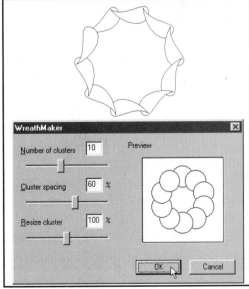

Wreath Recipes

133

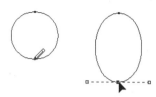

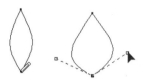

Try using the Bezier tool ![bezier] to elongate a circle before applying WreathMaker.

Once again, use the Bezier tool to alter a simple shape.

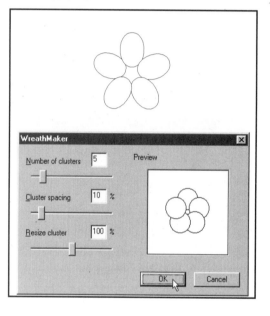

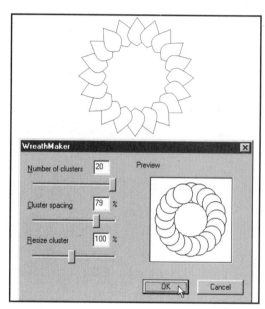

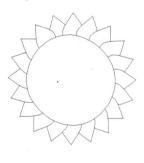

For the finishing touches, add a center, stem and leaves.

Add a circle in the middle to make this wreath a sunflower.

Wreath Recipes

For this wreath, start with a smaller simple oval.

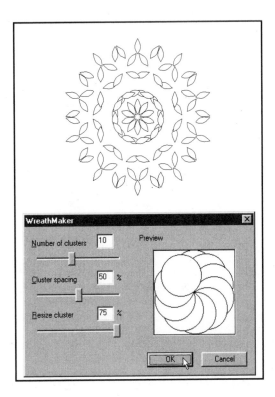

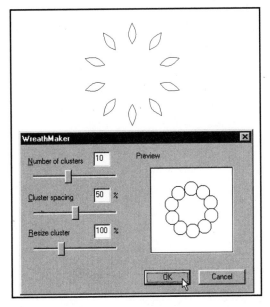

This wreath doesn't look like much now, but we can select the entire wreath and use WreathMaker on it again for a unique effect.

To make this wreath perfect, we'll have to rearrange the order of some of the simple ovals. *See:* LAYERING PATCHES.

For this next complex wreath we'll start with a small square.

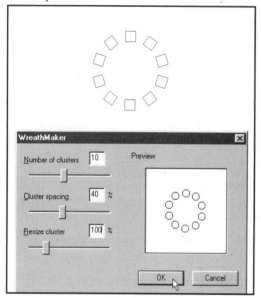

After deleting a few squares from the wreath, we'll apply WreathMaker to what's left, to get this complex wreath..

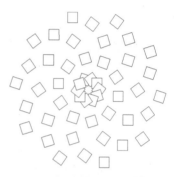

Then, delete a few squares from the wreath.

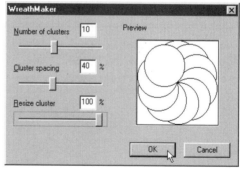

You can use the WreathMaker to make quilting patterns.For this example, we've kept the same WreathMaker settings and simply changed the shapes used.

There's virtually no limit to the number of original wreathes you can create with the WreathMaker!

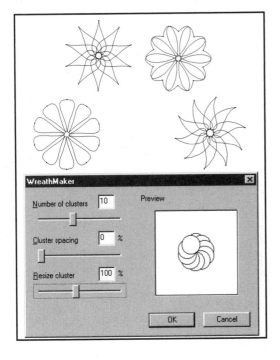

A quilt made out of WreathMaker wreathes.

Drawing a Vine with Leaves

To draw any appliqué patch, you must draw a complete closed patch (not just lines). It's easy to draw a rectangle, curve it to make a vine, then add leaves.

1 On the WORKTABLE menu, click Work on Block.

2 On the BLOCK menu, point to New Block, click PatchDraw.

3 Point to the Simple shape tool. Click the small black triangle on the tool. A toolbar showing shape options pops out.

4 Click the rectangle.

5 Pointing to your block's left edge, drag the mouse to the block's right edge and down slightly, forming a "stem-sized" rectangle as you draw. Release the mouse button *just* shy of the right edge of your block. You should now have a rectangular stem.

Note:
If your rectangle disappears after you draw it, it's because you ended your drawing a bit too far off the block. Redraw, ending your drawing *just* inside your block.

If you need to erase, click the EDIT menu, choose Undo.

6 Click the Bezier Edit tool.

7 Click one of the stem's long lines.

8 Click the little black square in the bottom-left corner of the Bezier Edit tool. The Edit Arc menu will appear.

9 Click toCurve. This will let you curve the line.

10 Click the other long stem line, to select it.

11 Click toCurve.

12 Holding down the SHIFT key, click the other line. Both lines should be selected. Release the SHIFT key.

Step 1

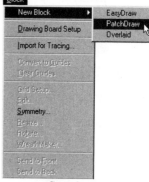

Step 2

Step 4

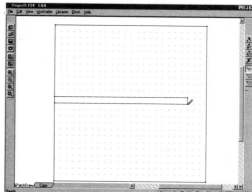

Step 5

You can't make an appliqué patch stem by drawing two lines across your block. You must draw the whole closed appliqué patch – this means drawing the stem's top and bottom, not just the long sides. So start by drawing a rectangle.

Step 6

Step 8

Steps 9 & 11

Drawing a Vine with Leaves

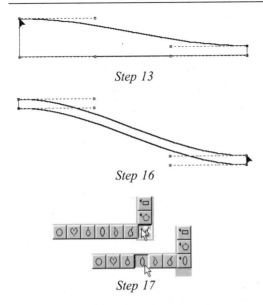

Step 13

Step 16

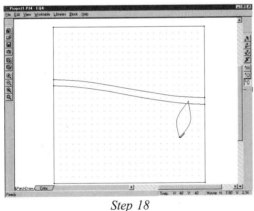

Step 17

Step 18

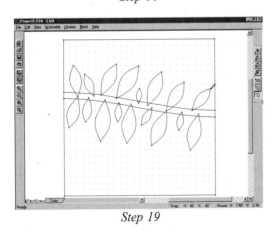

Step 19

13 Click the first node on the top line. Holding down the mouse, drag the node up about an inch. Note the arc/curve which is forming in the line.

14 Click the first node on the bottom line. Holding down the mouse, drag the node up about an inch so the curve matches the top line's arc.

15 Click on the second node of the bottom line. Holding down the mouse, drag the node down about an inch.

16 Click on the second node of the top line. Holding down the mouse, drag the node down about an inch.

You have created a simple vine. You may obviously make it more or less curvy. Now let's make some leaves for your vine.

17 Point to the Simple ovals tool. Click on the small black triangle in the top-left corner of the Simple ovals tool. A pop-out menu will appear with six shapes. Click one for your leaf shape.

18 Click on your line/vine where you want your leaf to begin. Holding down your mouse, drag the mouse away from the line an inch or two, depending on the leaf size you want.

19 Repeat step 18 to make as many leaves as you want.

 Notes & Tips

- **Keyboard shortcut – You can go back and forth from either the Bezier tool or the Line tool to the Bezier Edit tool by pressing the SPACEBAR.**

- **To add flowers to your vine, see:** DRAWING AN EASY APPLIQUE FLOWER.

- **To eliminate the background square, see:** ELIMINATING THE PATCHDRAW BACKGROUND.

Drawing a Vine with Leaves

139

Drawing an Applique Star

1　On the WORKTABLE menu, click Work on Block.

2　On the BLOCK menu, point to New Block, click PatchDraw.

3　On the Polygon tool, click the small black triangle in the top-left corner. A toolbar showing shape options pops out.

4　Click the octagon (the far-right shape).

5　Click, hold, and drag the mouse. You will see your polygon forming. Make the octagon any size you want.

6　Click the Bezier edit tool.

7　Click the top-horizontal segment. The line will be highlighted (appear darker).

8　On the Bezier edit tool, click the small black square in the bottom-left corner. An Edit Arc menu will pop-up.

9　On the Edit Arc menu, click Add. A node will be added to the line segment making it into two lines.

10　Click, hold, and drag either of the nodes beside the new node down about an inch.

11　Click, hold, and drag the other node beside the new node down about an inch (parallel to the other).

12　Click the bottom-horizontal segment. The line will be highlighted (appear darker).

13　On the Bezier edit tool, click the small black square in the bottom-left corner. The Edit Arc menu will pop-up again.

14　On the Edit Arc menu, click Add. A node will be added to the line segment making it into two lines.

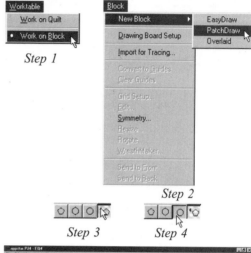

Step 1

Step 2

Step 3   *Step 4*

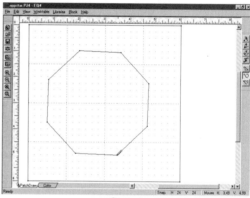

Step 5

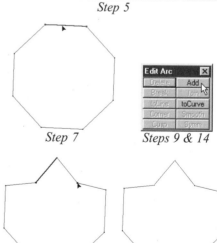

Step 7   *Steps 9 & 14*

Steps 10-11   *Step 12*

Drawing an Applique Star

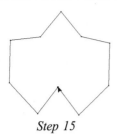

Step 15

Step 16

15 Click, hold, and drag the new node up about an inch.

16 Click, hold, and drag both of the side nodes in approximately an inch.

At this point you have the basic outline of a star. You can move nodes if you want to further reshape the star.

Notes & Tips

- You made a five-point star for this recipe. However, you can add more points to the star by adding nodes/segments from the Edit Arc pop-up menu.
- You can resize your star. See: RESIZING A BLOCK PATCH.
- You can add stripes (using the rectangle shape) to make a flag block.
- There are blocks in the library with stars in them. However, being able to draw stars and other shapes by yourself introduces you to all of the drawing possibilities of EQ4, makes each patch personal, and it's fun!

Drawing an Applique Star

Drawing an Applique Dove

1 On the WORKTABLE menu, click Work on Block.

2 On the BLOCK menu, point to New Block, click PatchDraw.

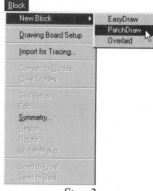

Step 1

Step 2

3 On the Simple shape tool, click the small black triangle in the top-left corner. A toolbar showing shape options pops out.

4 Click the rectangle (the far-right shape).

5 Click, hold, and drag the mouse. You will see your simple shape forming. Make the rectangle any size you want.

6 Click the Bezier edit tool.
You will be adding three nodes to the rectangle to help shape it into a dove.

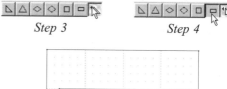

Step 3   *Step 4*

7 Click the top-horizontal segment. The line will be highlighted (appear darker).

8 On the Bezier edit tool, click the small black square in the bottom-left corner. An Edit Arc menu will pop-up.

9 On the Edit Arc menu, click Add. A node will be added to the line segment making it into two lines.

10 Repeat steps 7-9 for the bottom and right side of the rectangle. You will now have 7 total nodes.

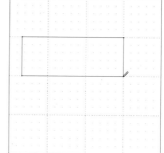

Step 5

11 Click, hold, and drag the new node on the right side of the rectangle up so it is almost even with the top of the rectangle and to the right ½ inch (this is creating the top of the beak).

12 Click, hold, and drag the new node on top of the rectangle down about ½ inch.

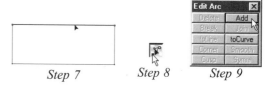

Step 7   *Step 8*   *Step 9*

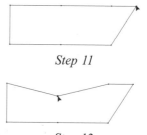

Step 11

Step 12

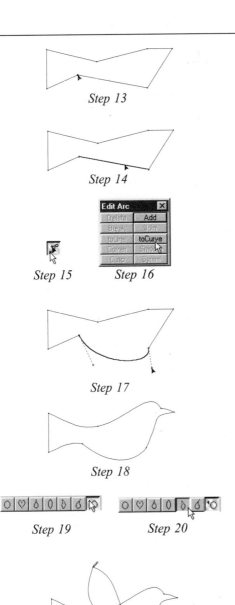

Step 13

Step 14

Step 15   Step 16

Step 17

Step 18

Step 19   Step 20

Step 21

13 Click, hold, and drag the new node on the lower side of the rectangle ¾ inches to the left and up ½ inch.

Your bird probably does not look much like a dove at this point, so we're going to curve and shape some of the lines. It is helpful having a picture of the shape you're trying to create nearby to help you form it.

14 Click on the bottom-right line so it is highlighted (appears darker).

15 On the Bezier edit tool, click the small black square in the bottom-left corner so the Edit Arc menu will pop-up.

16 On the Edit Arc menu, click toCurve. The segment will now have two handle nodes.

17 Click, hold, and drag the handle nodes down to create the bird's breast.

18 Repeat steps 14-17 for all other lines except the left vertical line. For each line (now a curve) drag the handle nodes whichever direction they need to go to form the dove's body.

We can't forget the bird's wing.

19 On the Simple ovals tool, click the small black triangle in the top-left corner. A toolbar showing shape options pops out.

20 Click the shape second to the right.

21 While holding down the mouse, drag the cursor from the center of the body above and to the left. Release the mouse and you will have formed the wing. Now your bird can fly!

At this point you can:

- Give the dove another wing and send it to the back. See: LAYERING PATCHES.

- Have the bird holding a flower in its beak. See: DRAWING AN EASY APPLIQUE FLOWER.

- Have many birds in the block by cloning the original dove. See: COPYING PATCHES.

Drawing an Applique Dove

Drawing an Applique Tulip

1 On the WORKTABLE menu, click Work on Block.

2 On the BLOCK menu, point to New Block, click PatchDraw.

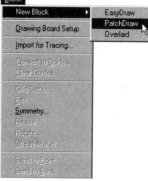

Step 1

Step 2

3 On the Simple shape tool, click the small black triangle in the top-left corner. A toolbar showing shape options pops out.

4 Click one of the diamond shapes. (For this recipe we'll use the third shape from the left.)

5 Click, hold, and drag the mouse. You will see your simple shape forming. Make the diamond any size you want.

Step 3   *Step 4*

6 Click the Bezier edit tool.

7 Click, hold, and drag one of the diamond's side nodes up so it is parallel with the top diamond node.

8 Repeat step 7 for the node on the diamond's other side. The top of the diamond will now look like two line segments making up a single straight line with a node in the middle and on both ends.

9 Click one of the diamond's top two line segments. The section will be highlighted (appear darker).

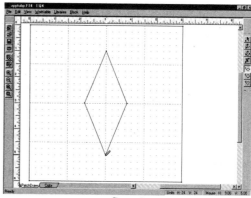

Step 5

10 On the Bezier edit tool, click the small black square in the bottom-left corner. An Edit Arc menu will pop-up.

11 On the Edit Arc menu, click Add. A node will be added to the line segment making it into two lines.

12 Repeat step 11 for the other top line segment. There will be five nodes across the top making up four small lines or segments.

Steps 7-9

13 Click one of the new nodes (either the second or fourth node in the top line). Hold and drag the node (half an inch)

Step 11

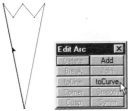

Steps 13-14

Steps 15-16

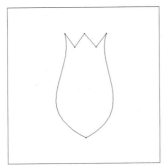

Steps 17-18

below the other nodes and release.

14 Repeat step 13 with the other new node. You will now have three points (or petals) for your tulip.

15 Click one of the sides of the diamond. The side will be highlighted (appear darker).

16 On the Edit Arc pop-up menu, click toCurve. The segment will now have two handle nodes.

17 Click, hold, and drag the top-handle node slightly inward to shape the tulip.

18 Click, hold, and drag the bottom-handle node down and outward to complete the form of the tulip.

19 Repeat steps 15-18 for the other side of the diamond. When you are done you will have made a tulip. Good job!

At this point you can:

- Add a vine to your tulip. See: DRAWING A VINE WITH LEAVES.

- Make copies of your tulip. See: COPYING PATCHES.

- Resize your tulip. See: RESIZING A PATCH.

- Color your tulip block. See: COLORING A BLOCK.

- Place your tulip block into a quilt layout. See: SETTING BLOCKS INTO A QUILT LAYOUT.

The finished block

Drawing an Applique Tulip

Drawing an Applique Bow

1 On the WORKTABLE menu, click Work on Block.

2 On the BLOCK menu, point to New Block, click PatchDraw.

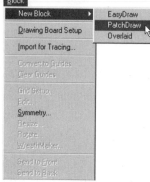

Step 1

3 On the Polygon tool, click the small black triangle in the top-left corner. A toolbar showing shape options pops out.

4 Click the octagon (the far-right shape).

5 Click, hold, and drag the mouse on the block. You will see your polygon forming. Make the octagon any size you want. (However, for this recipe we will begin the octagon at the 1½-inch marking on the top and side rulers. We will release the rectangle on the 4½-inch marking on both rulers.)

Step 2

Step 3   *Step 4*

6 Click the Bezier Edit tool.

7 Click, hold, and drag the top node straight down 1½ inches.

8 Click, hold, and drag the node at the 4½-inch side ruler marking and the 1½-inch top ruler marking 1 inch to the right and 1¼ inches up.

9 Click, hold, and drag the other node at the 4½-inch side ruler marking 1 inch to the left and 1¼ inches up. Both sides of the shape should mirror each other.

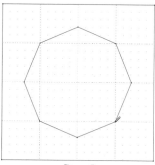

Step 5

10 Click the lower-left vertical segment. It will be highlighted (appear darker).

11 On the Bezier edit tool, click the small black square in the bottom-left corner. An Edit Arc menu will pop-up.

12 On the Edit Arc pop-up menu click Add. A new node will appear and the segment will be divided into two lines.

13 Click, hold, and drag the new node both down and to the left one inch.

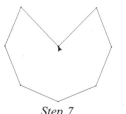

Step 7

Steps 8 and 9

Step 10   *Step 12*

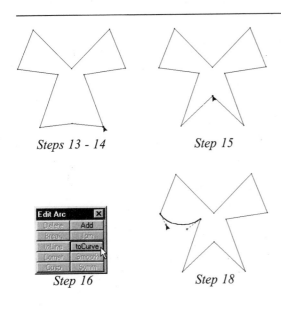

Steps 13 - 14 *Step 15*

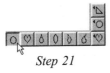

Step 16 *Step 18*

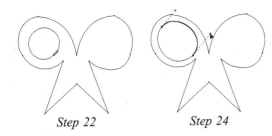

Step 21

Step 22 *Step 24*

Step 25

14 Repeat steps11-13 for the lower-right vertical segment. However, drag it down and to the right.

15 Click, hold, and drag the lower-center node (it's between the two new bottom segments) up one inch.

Hopefully you can see the bow taking shape. We are now going to create the loops of the bow by curving lines.

16 Click any of the top 6 lines so it is highlighted (appears darker).

17 On the Edit Arc pop-up menu click toCurve. The segment will now have two handle nodes.

18 Click, hold, and drag the handle nodes out to begin creating the bow's loop.

19 Repeat steps 16-18 for the five remaining top lines.

20 On the Simple ovals tool, click the small black triangle in the top-left corner. A toolbar showing shape options pops out.

21 Click the circle (the farthest left shape).

22 While holding down the mouse, drag the cursor inside one of the loops to form a circle. The circle is what will create the illusion of the loop being open.

23 Click the Bezier Edit tool.

24 Click, hold, and drag the circle's handle nodes to reshape the circle to match the form of the loop.

25 Repeat steps 21-24 for the other loop. You've created a bow, good job!

At this point you can:

• Reshape the bow ends by adding curves.

• Add a square under the bow to create a present or package. See: LAYERING PATCHES

• Add more wavy ribbons to the loop by adding lines and curving them.

Drawing an Applique Bow

Drawing a Complex Leaf

The key to this recipe is to imagine a leaf or look at a picture of a real leaf and see if you can duplicate it.

1   On the WORKTABLE menu, click Work on Block.

2   On the BLOCK menu, point to New Block, click PatchDraw.

3   On the Polygon tool, click the small black triangle in the top-left corner. A toolbar showing shape options pops out.

4   Click the pentagon (the five-sided shape).

5   Click, hold, and drag the mouse on your block to draw a pentagon. Make the pentagon any size you want. However, don't make it so big that any sides are outside the block border.

6   Click the Bezier edit tool.

7   Point to a node (black box) at the pentagon's bottom, then click, hold and drag the node toward another node, so you have two nodes close together at the bottom of the block, about the width of the leaf stem. You're beginning to form the leaf.

8   Click on the small black square in the bottom-left corner of the Bezier Edit tool. An Edit Node menu will pop up.
You are now going to add several new lines/nodes (by breaking original lines in half).

9   Click on a long line on your drawing. It will appear highlighted (darker). Now two options will appear highlighted on the Edit Arc menu.

10 On the Edit Arc menu, click Add. A new node will appear at the midpoint of the selected line dividing the original line into two.

11 Point to the center of the selected line. Click, hold, and drag the node in or out to

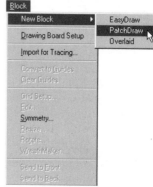

Step 1

Step 2

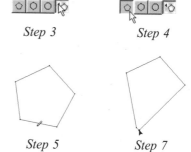

Step 3   *Step 4*

Step 5   *Step 7*

Step 8

Steps 9 and 10

148

Drawing a Complex Leaf

Step 12

Step 14

Step 16

The finished leaf

help shape the leaf.

12 Repeat steps 9-11 many times. Continue dividing line segments and moving nodes.

Next, you'll turn these straight lines to curved lines.

13 Click on a line you want to curve.

14 On the Edit Arc menu, click toCurve. Nothing happens to the straight line, but two handle nodes are added.

15 Click, hold, and drag one of the handle nodes and notice the curve it starts to make.

16 Move both handle nodes until the line has an arc that looks like the leaf's curve.

17 Repeat steps 13-16 as many times as you want, to curve lines.

When you finish adding, moving, and curving lines you will have a shape that forms a leaf. This method of adding nodes and curving lines will help you form almost any patch shape.

Notes & Tips

- The more lines you "Add," the easier it is to form and then curve a leaf (or any shape).
- If you decide later you don't want a line to be curved, click on the line and on the Edit Arc menu, click toLine.
- By using the pentagon or any other shape to form the leaf, you know the patch is closed.

Drawing a Complex Leaf

149

Drawing a Basket of Flowers

To combine pieced and applique patches in the same block, work on an Overlaid block.

1   On the WORKTABLE menu, click Work on Block.

Step 1

2   On the BLOCK menu, point to New Block, click Overlaid. You will see a drawing worktable, with 3 tabs – Pieced, Applique and Color. The Pieced tab will be on top, with the EasyDraw tools.

3   Click the Line tool. (It may already be selected.)

4   Draw a simple basket, as shown in the picture.

    OR

    Get a pieced basket block from the Block Library, into your Sketchbook, open the Sketchbook and click on the Edit button.

5   Click the Applique tab (at screen bottom). The PatchDraw tools appear. The basket needs some flowers.

6   Click the small black triangle on the Simple ovals tool. You'll see shape choices.

7   Click the circle.

8   Draw some circles within circles to make simple flowers. (Click, hold and drag to make a circle.)

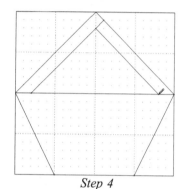

Step 2

Step 3

Step 4

Step 5

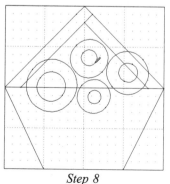

Step 6   Step 7

Step 8

Step 9

Step 10

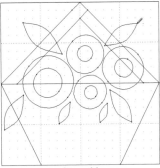

Step 11

Step 12

9 To add leaves, click the small black triangle on the Simple ovals tool.

10 Click the leaf.

11 Draw some leaves. (Click, hold and drag to make a leaf.)

12 Click the Color tab (at screen bottom). The layering of patches will appear obvious here. To make a patch appear in front or in back of another patch see: LAYERING PATCHES.

Notes & Tips

- When working on the block, you can edit EasyDraw lines on the Pieced tab, and edit PatchDraw lines on the Applique tab.

- Pieced patches will always be behind applique patches, just as they will be when you sew the block.

- To draw a scalloped flower, see: DRAWING AN EASY APPLIQUÉ FLOWER.

Drawing a Basket of Flowers

151

Part 9
Quilt Recipes

Part 9
Quilt Recipes

Making a Strip Quilt

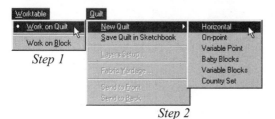

Step 1

Step 2

Step 3

Steps 4-6

Step 7

Step 9

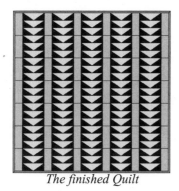

The finished Quilt

This basic quilt layout recipe will work with many blocks to make a variety of strip quilts.

1 On the WORKTABLE menu, click Work on Quilt.

2 On the QUILT menu, point to New Quilt, click Horizontal.

3 Click on the Layout tab.

4 In Number of blocks, click the up and down arrows to make Horizontal 5 and Vertical 7.

5 In Size of blocks, click, hold, and drag both slider bars to make Width and Height read 12.00.

6 In Sashing, click, hold, and drag the Width slider bar to read 4.00; make the Height slider bar read 0.00. Your quilt now has strips of vertical sashes.

7 Click the Layer 1 tab.

8 Get a block from the Block Library.

Note:

  See: GETTING BLOCKS FROM THE LIBRARY.
  We suggest trying blocks from the 1 Classic Pieced / Simple Blocks style.

9 Click the Set tool.

10 Click any block in the Sketchbook Blocks box.

11 Holding down the CTRL key, click on any block space (not sash strip block) in your quilt.

12 Click the Plain Block tool.

13 Click a color or fabric swatch in the palette.

14 Holding down the CTRL key, click on any sash block space in your quilt.

15 Holding down the CTRL key, click on any border strip to color your border.

Making a Strip Quilt

Making an Amish Quilt

Diamond in the Square

Follow the steps below to make a Diamond in the Square layout – a traditional Amish quilt style featuring a central on-point square surrounded by borders.

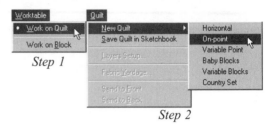

Step 1

Step 2

1   On the WORKTABLE menu, click Work on Quilt.

2   On the Quilt menu, point to New Quilt, click On-point.

3   Click the Layout tab. The On-point layout pop-up window will appear.

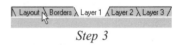

Step 3

4   In Number of blocks, click the up and down arrows to make both Horizontal and Vertical 1.

5   In Size of blocks, click, hold, and drag the slider bar until it reads 48.00.

6   In Sashing, click, hold, and drag the slider bar so it reads 6.00.

Note:
You can also move the slider bar by clicking right on the bar (not the slider). This "jumps" the slider ¼ for each click. Or drag the mouse over the number to highlight it, then type in the number.

Steps 4 - 6   *Step 7*

7   Click the Borders tab.

8   In Number of borders, click Add. The "Quilt has 2 borders" now. (The outer border will appear highlighted or darkened).

9   Under Style, click the down arrow to drop the list of border styles. Click Corner Blocks.

10 Under Size of border, click, hold, and drag the slider bar for the Left, Top, Right, and Bottom sides until all read 20.00.

Steps 8 - 10

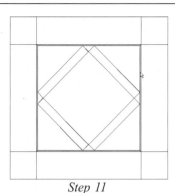

Step 11

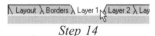

Steps 12 and 13   *Step 14*

11 Click the inside border of your quilt. It will appear highlighted (darkened).

12 Under Style, click the down arrow. Click Corner Blocks.

13 Under Size of border, click, hold, and drag the slider bar for the Left, Top, Right, and Bottom sides until all read 6.00.

Note:
Blocks in border is not highlighted for either border since there are no blocks in this style of border.

14 Click the Layer 1 tab. You will see the layout for a basic Diamond in Square Amish quilt.

15 Click the Paintbrush tool and color your quilt with whatever fabrics and/or colors you wish. See: COLORING A QUILT.

Making an Amish Quilt

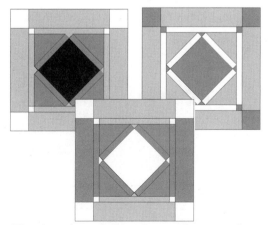

There's no limit to the color combinations for your finished quilt!

Making a Double Wedding Ring Quilt

Before you start the quilt layout you need to copy two blocks from the library: Double Wedding Ring and the Quarter Wedding Ring. These blocks are in the Block Library's EQ Libraries in the Classic Pieced Library under the Classics style. To get these blocks, see GETTING BLOCKS FROM THE LIBRARY.

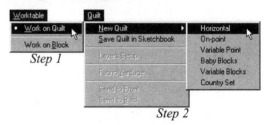

Step 1

Step 2

1   On the WORKTABLE menu, click Work on Quilt.

2   On the QUILT menu, point to New Quilt, click Horizontal.

Step 3

3   Click the Layout tab. The Horizontal layout box will appear.

4   In Number of blocks, click the up and down arrows to make both Horizontal and Vertical 6.

5   In Size of blocks, click, hold, and drag both slider bars until they read 8.00.

6   In Sashing, click, hold, and drag the slider bar so both Width and Height read 0.00.

Note:
You can click directly on the bar (not the slider) to "jump" the slider ¼ for each click. Or drag the mouse over the number to highlight it, then type in the number.

Steps 4-6　　　　*Step 7*

7   Click the Borders tab.

8   Under Style, click the down arrow to drop the list of border styles. Click Tile Squares.

9   In Blocks in border, click the up and down arrows to make Horizontal 6. EQ4 will automatically calculate the size required, and number of blocks needed to fit along a vertical side.

Note:
For any border that has tiles (or blocks) you can add tiles to the horizontal side ranging from 1 to 24.

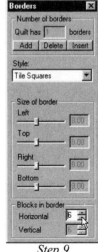

Step 8　　　　*Step 9*

10   Click the Layer 1 tab. You will have 64

Step 10

158

Step 11

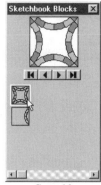

Step 12

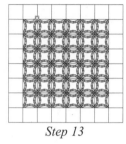

Step 13

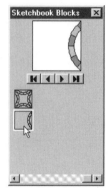

Step 14

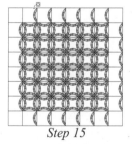

Step 15

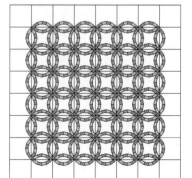

A finished Double Wedding Ring quilt.

equally-sized blocks. (Remember, the outside edge blocks are your border.)

11 Click the Set tool. You will see your two library blocks.

12 Click the Double Wedding Ring block.

13 Holding down the CTRL key, click on any block in the center of your quilt layout (not the outside borders). The block will appear in every space. The edge blocks are not completed wedding rings, so we need to add the quarter ring.

14 Click the Quarter Wedding Ring block.

15 Holding down the CTRL key, click on any tile/block in the border *except* for a corner. The Quarter Wedding Ring block will complete the wedding rings on the left side of the quilt. But, this block needs to be rotated on the other three sides of the quilt to complete the wedding ring.

16 Click the Rotate tool.

17 Click each Quarter Wedding Ring block on the top once, twice on the right side, and three times on the bottom. When you are finished rotating the blocks your double wedding ring quilt will be completed.

💡 **Notes & Tips** ─────────

• **You may want to color the outside of the quarter wedding ring block white to emphasize the scalloped edge.**

Making a Double Wedding Ring Quilt

159

Coloring a Flower Garden Grid

1 On the WORKTABLE menu, click Work on Quilt.

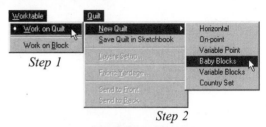

Step 1

2 On the QUILT menu, point to New Quilt, click Baby Blocks.

Step 2

3 Click the Layout tab. The Baby Block layout pop-up window will appear.

Step 3

4 In Number of blocks, click the up and down arrows to make Horizontal 9 and Vertical 6.

5 In Size of blocks, click, hold, and drag the slider bar until it reads 8.00.

Steps 4-5

6 Click the Borders tab.
We're going to keep the one original mitered border, so nothing needs to be changed on the top half.

Step 6

7 Under Size of border, click, hold, and drag the slider bar for the Left, Top, Right, and Bottom sides until all read 2.00.

Note:

> Slider bar shortcuts – click right on the bar (not the slider rectangle). This "jumps" the slider bar ¼" with each click.
>
> **OR**
>
> Click, hold, and drag your cursor across the size number, to highlight it, then type the size you want.

8 Click Layer 1.
We are going to color the blocks to create a Grandmother's Flower Garden (six hexagons surrounding a center hexagon).

9 Click the Paintbrush tool.

Step 7

Step 8

Step 9

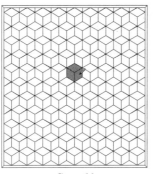

Step 10   *Step 11*

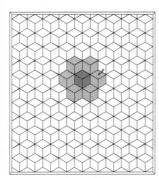

Step 12   *Step 13*

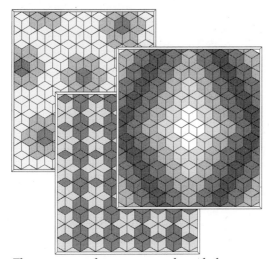

There are countless ways to color a baby blocks quilt.

10   Click a Fabric & Color swatch

11   Start by coloring a center "block" or hexagon. This "block" consists of three diamonds. Color all 3 diamonds the same color.

12   Click on a different color.

13   Color the six hexagons surrounding the block you just colored. In total, you will color 18 patches. You will have your first Grandmother's Flower Garden.

14   Repeat steps 10-13 as many times as you want, to make more Grandmother's Flower Gardens.

You can connect them side by side or one on top of the other. You can make a straight horizontal line of Grandmother's Flower Gardens, but a vertical line must slightly zig zag or go diagonally. You can also leave space between the flower gardens or separate them with a star or another shape.

💡 **Notes & Tips** ───────────

- **Try coloring the blocks in different formations to create different patterns such as: stars (six adjacent diamonds with the same center point); a flower that expands over the whole quilt (start by coloring one hexagon as the center and continue surrounding it with circles of hexagons); entire scenes (make up your own pictures); or, color all of the blocks to make a traditional tumbling blocks quilt (each side of a block should be a different color).**
- **If you hold down the ALT key while you color a block it will color every other similar block.**
- **If you hold down the CTRL key while you color a block it will color every similar block.**

Coloring a Flower Garden Grid

Making "Prairie Point" Borders

The border styles called Triangle Out and Triangle In are handy for making instant "Prairie Point" and New York Beauty borders. True Prairie Point borders are made with fabric squares folded into triangles and inserted to edge a border. New York Beauty quilts are often bordered with long spiky triangles, re-popularized today by designers such as Karen K. Stone. To create these borders in EQ4, you must first have a quilt layout. If you do not have a layout showing on the worktable, start at step 1 below. If you do have a layout, start at step 3.

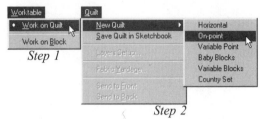

Step 1

Step 2

For our example, we'll be using an On-point layout.

Step 3

1   On the WORKTABLE menu, click Work on Quilt.

2   On the QUILT menu, point to New Quilt, click any layout style. Then to make a quilt border, follow the steps below.

3   Click the Borders tab. The Borders box will appear.

4   Click the down arrow on the Style box. A list of border style choices drops down.

5   Click Triangle Out or Triangle In

Note:
These two styles produce the same effect, being different only at the corners.

6   Under Blocks in border, click the Horizontal and Vertical up arrows to put 24 in the box. Each click puts another triangle in the border.

7   Under Size of Border, click, hold, and drag the Left, Top, Right, Bottom slider bars if you wish your triangles to be longer.

Note:
For "Prairie Point" borders, we suggest border widths between 1.00" and 2.50."

For New York Beauty borders, we suggest border widths between 4.00" and 11.00."

These dimensions, of course, will vary depending on your quilt's overall size.

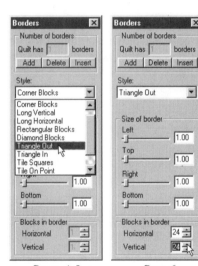

Steps 4-5   *Step 6*

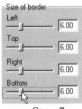

Step 7

Step 8

Step 9

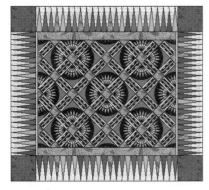

A completed New York Beauty quilt.

8   Click the Layer 1 tab when you are finished creating your border outline.

9   Click the Paintbrush tool. The Fabrics & Colors palette appears.

10 Color your border triangles by clicking on a swatch in the palette, then clicking on a triangle in your border.

Note:
CTRL + click: To color all "in" or "out" pointing triangles in your border at once, hold down the CTRL key and click on a border triangle.

ALT + click: To color all "in" or "out" pointing triangles in one border strip (top, bottom, left or right) hold down the ALT key and click on a border triangle.

 Notes & Tips —————————————

• To print a border triangle, click the Select tool, click on the border triangle, click FILE on the main menu bar, click Print. The Size from quilt box will be checked. Click the Print button. EQ4 will print a diamond. Your triangle will be half that diamond.

• To insert a border between another, click the quilt border you want to insert a border in front of. The border turns gray, showing it is selected. Click the Insert button. A mitered border will be inserted. To change the border style, do step 4 above.

• You can place, rotate and flip blocks in a border just as in a quilt. If you want to set a block into a triangular border block you can do so.

Making "Prairie Point" Borders

Part 10
Index

Index

The EQ4 Quick Reference Tool Guide

Main Tools:

- Create a New project
- Open a Project
- Save
- Export Snapshot
- View Sketchbook
- Save in Sketchbook
- Zoom In
- Zoom Out
- Refresh Screen
- Fit to Window

Layout Tools:

- Select tool
- Set tool
- Plain Block tool
- Rotate tool
- Flip tool
- Adjust tool
- Paintbrush tool
- Spraycan tool
- Swap tool
- Fussy Cut tool

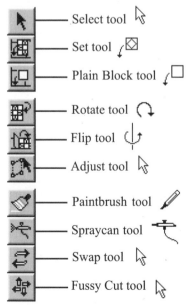

EasyDraw Tools:

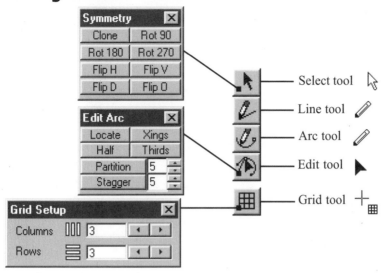

Symmetry

Clone	Rot 90
Rot 180	Rot 270
Flip H	Flip V
Flip D	Flip 0

— Select tool

— Line tool

— Arc tool

— Edit tool

— Grid tool

Edit Arc

Locate	Xings
Half	Thirds
Partition	5
Stagger	5

Grid Setup

| Columns | 3 |
| Rows | 3 |

PatchDraw Tools:

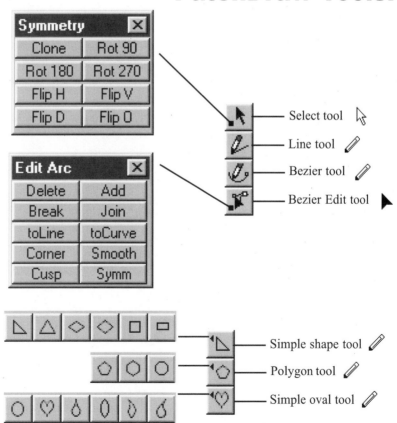

Symmetry

Clone	Rot 90
Rot 180	Rot 270
Flip H	Flip V
Flip D	Flip 0

— Select tool

— Line tool

— Bezier tool

— Bezier Edit tool

Edit Arc

Delete	Add
Break	Join
toLine	toCurve
Corner	Smooth
Cusp	Symm

— Simple shape tool

— Polygon tool

— Simple oval tool